HOMEMADE HEALTHY DOG FOOD COOKBOOK

ANDREA CURREY

TABLE OF CONTENTS

ABOUT AUTHOR

Andrea Curry's journey with dogs began in the idyllic landscapes of Massachusetts, where she was born and raised. Growing up, dogs of all breeds, sizes, and temperaments were not just pets but integral parts of her life. They were her playmates, loyal companions, and trusted protectors, shaping her love and understanding of these beautiful creatures.

Over the years, Andrea's passion for dogs has only strengthened. Now, she is not only the wonderful owner of four remarkable pets - two adorable dachshunds, a majestic Rottweiler, and a devoted Doberman — but also a true expert in healthy dog nutrition.

Collaborating with leading experts in veterinary science, dietetics, and culinary arts, Andrea has tirelessly worked to develop optimal recipes for balanced homemade meals for the health and happiness of her furry friends. Her constant experiments and research have yielded excellent results — improving pets' health and prolonging their active and joyful lives.

Andrea has become an expert in dog nutrition and a kind advisor to all who share her passion for these beautiful creatures. Her friends, neighbors, and acquaintances — all turn to her for advice on improving their pets' diets. Her knowledge and experience have helped countless furry friends and their loving owners.

In her book, Andrea has compiled all her rich experience and knowledge. "Homemade Healthy Dog Food Cookbook" is not just a recipe collection — it's a culinary journey into the world of care and love for one's pets, where every page is filled with care, love, and knowledge. It's an excellent guide to the world of dog nutrition, promising a healthy, long, and happy life to every furry friend in need of their owner's care and attention.

WHY HOMEMADE DOG FOOD?

Have you ever found yourself gazing into the sparkling eyes of your furry best friend and wondering if there's more you could do for their health and happiness? You're not alone. Many pet parents are switching to homemade dog food, driven by love, concern, and the culinary thrill of creating something nourishing with their own hands. But why exactly should you consider whipping up your dog's meals at home? Let's dive into the delightful world of homemade dog food and discover its bountiful benefits.

Tailored Nutrition at Its Finest. Every dog is unique. From the bouncy little terriers to the stoic great Danes, each has its own dietary needs based on size, age, activity level, and health conditions. Store-bought food often takes a one-size-fits-all approach, but homemade meals can perfectly suit your dog's individual requirements. You can become a chef specialized in canine cuisine who can tweak every nutrient and flavor for your furry friend.

Quality Control You Can Trust. You see every ingredient in the pot when you cook your dog's meals. This transparency is reassuring in an age where recalls and questionable ingredients frequently make headlines. By choosing homemade, you eliminate the guesswork and gain peace of mind knowing exactly what your dog is eating—fresh, wholesome ingredients with no hidden nasties. There is no doubt that it benefits your dog in the long run.

Forge a Deeper Bond. Cooking is an act of love, whether it's for your family or your dog. Preparing your dog's meals is a daily ritual that shows your pet that it is valued and cared for, and believe it or not, dogs do sense this care. The wagging tail and eager eyes at mealtime say it all.

Bursting with Flavor. Let's remember the taste! Homemade dog food often tastes better than its commercial counterparts. After all, what would you prefer—a meal made with fresh chicken and vegetables or something rehydrated from a dusty kibble bag? Chances are, your dog will have an opinion on this, too. Watching your dog enjoy their food can be a joy, adding an extra sprinkle of delight to mealtimes. After all, food prepared with love tastes distinctly better, doesn't it? This is true for humans and canines alike!

Economically Wise. Believe it or not, making dog food at home can also be cost-effective. Buying ingredients in bulk, utilizing garden veggies, or repurposing safe leftovers can reduce the overall expenses tied to dog care. With careful planning, homemade dog food can be a financially savvy option that enhances your dog's health and saves on future vet bills.

Creativity in the Kitchen. Cooking for your dog encourages creativity in the kitchen. You'll learn to mix proteins, balance grains and veggies, and even concoct special treats. It's a culinary adventure! Think of the joy of creating something special for your pet, and every day, you'll have a tail-wagging audience grateful for your healthy creations.

A Healthier, Happier Dog. Perhaps the most compelling reason to cook homemade dog food is the difference it can make to your pet's health. Owners often report shinier coats, more energy, and better overall health in their pets after switching to homemade food. This boost in their well-being indicates the diet's effectiveness, leading to fewer diseases, a more vibrant lifestyle, and more wagging tails.

So, why cook homemade dog food? It's a joyful, fulfilling journey that benefits both you and your beloved pet. It strengthens the bond, ensures a healthier diet, and can be a lot of fun. Unleash your inner chef and watch your dog thrive—happy cooking!

CHAPTER 1

BASICS OF
DOG NUTRITION

mineral has a role, from Vitamin A improving vision to calcium strengthening bones and iron carrying oxygen in the blood. Think of them as the special effects team that enhances your dog's performance and appearance, ensuring they shine inside and out. By understanding their roles, you can empower yourself to make informed decisions about your dog's diet.

It is vital to include a variety of food sources in the diet to ensure your dog receives all the essential vitamins and minerals as they work best together.

1.4. THE ROLE OF HYDRATION IN DOG NUTRITION

Water's importance in living creatures' lives is difficult to overestimate. Water does more than quench thirst; it aids digestion, helps absorb nutrients, regulates body temperature, and flushes out toxins. It keeps your dog's joints lubricated and their tissues healthy. Always ensure your dog can access fresh water, mainly if its diet includes dry food. A good "rule of paw" is that a dog should drink approximately one ounce of water per pound of body weight daily. Remember that wet foods can also help meet your dog's hydration needs.

1.5. REQUIREMENTS FOR PORTION SIZE, FEEDING FREQUENCY, AND CALORIES BASED ON SIZE, AGE, AND ACTIVITY

Feeding your dog isn't just about filling a bowl; it's about tailoring their diet to their life's blueprint. Puppies, for instance, require more calories and frequent meals for their growing bodies, while seniors might need fewer calories to avoid weight gain.

- Puppies typically thrive on 3 to 4 meals a day.
- Adult dogs usually do well with 2 meals a day.
- Senior dogs may continue on two meals or switch to one depending on their activity level and health.

Caloric needs vary dramatically depending on your dog's size, age, and activity level. A sprightly border collie herding sheep may burn twice as many calories as a serene Shih Tzu patrolling the living room.

Small breed pups may need small, frequent meals to stabilize their energy levels, while larger breeds might manage with two hearty meals daily.

Caloric needs are a dance between too much and too little, influenced by activity levels and metabolic rates. Observing your dog's weight and energy are your cues to adjust their diet choreography as needed.

Daily Food Intake Table

Dog Size	Age	Activity Level	Daily Calories (kcal)
Small	Puppy	High	600
	Adult	Low	300
		Moderate	400
		High	500
	Senior	Low	200
Medium	Puppy	High	1000
	Adult	Low	700
		Moderate	900
		High	1100
	Senior	Low	500
Large	Puppy	High	1500
	Adult	Low	1000
		Moderate	1300
		High	1600
	Senior	Low	800
X-Large	Puppy	High	2000
	Adult	Low	1600
		Moderate	2000
		High	2400
	Senior	Low	1200

Dog Size Categories and Weight Ranges

- Small: 5-20 lbs
- Medium: 20-50 lbs
- Large: 50-90 lbs
- X-Large: Over 90 lbs

Dog Age Categories

- Puppy: 0-1 year
- Adult: 1-7 years
- Senior: Over 7 years

Activity Levels

- Low: Mostly inactive, light daily activity
- Moderate: Regular exercise, active 30-60 minutes daily
- High: Very active, over 60 minutes of vigorous exercise daily

Daily Food Intake Table

Age Group	Activity Level	Protein (%)	Fat (%)	Carbohydrates (%)
Puppy & Active Adults	High	30	20	50
Adults	Moderate	28	18	54
Seniors & Low Active Adults	High	30	20	50

- Puppies require more frequent meals and higher calories, protein, and fat per pound of body weight due to their growth needs.
- Adult dogs have varying caloric needs based on activity levels; more active dogs require more calories and protein.
- Senior dogs generally need fewer calories, protein, and fat due to lower activity levels and slower metabolism but still require nutrient-rich food to maintain health.

Portion sizes generally increase with the dog's size but are adjusted based on the dog's activity level and age.

Puppies typically receive a higher feeding frequency to support their rapid growth and metabolism, while adults and seniors are usually fed twice a day.

This table serves as a general guideline, and specific needs can vary based on the dog's health, metabolism, and other factors. It's always best to consult a veterinarian to tailor feeding practices to a dog's individual needs.

Adjust portion sizes and meal frequencies constantly to maintain optimal body weight and support your dog's overall health and energy needs.

Let the culinary adventure begin! Remember, the ultimate goal is a happy, healthy pet who enjoys each meal with gusto and lives an excellent, vibrant life by your side.

CHAPTER 2

TRANSITIONING TO HOMEMADE FOOD

2.1. HOW TO SAFELY SWITCH YOUR DOG TO HOMEMADE FOOD

Transitioning to homemade food isn't an overnight switch; it's a smooth process that respects your dog's eating habits while introducing new flavors and textures.

This chapter provides a step-by-step guide to safely transition your dog to homemade food, including the recommended transition period and a daily feeding schedule.

First, consult a vet to understand any specific nutritional needs or restrictions your dog may have. Once you have a plan, introduce homemade food gradually. Start by mixing a small amount of the homemade meal with the dog's current food, slowly increasing the proportion of homemade food.

A gradual transition is crucial when introducing new food to your dog's diet, especially homemade food. Sudden dietary changes can cause digestive issues such as diarrhea, vomiting, or constipation. A slow transition allows your dog's digestive system to adapt to the new food without causing distress.

Recommended Transition Period. The recommended transition period for switching to homemade dog food is typically about 10 days. This timeframe can be adjusted based on your dog's specific needs and reactions to the new diet. Monitor your dog closely for signs of digestive upset or food intolerance, such as excessive gas, bloating, or changes in stool consistency. If any of these occur, it may be necessary to extend the transition period.

The Transition Process: A Daily Guide. Below is a table outlining the daily transition from commercial dog food to homemade food. The percentage of homemade food gradually increases each day while the percentage of commercial dog food decreases.

Day	Commercial Dog Food (%)	Homemade Food (%)
1	90	10
2	80	20
3	70	30
4	60	40
5	50	50
6	40	60
7	30	70
8	20	80
9	10	90
10	0	100

2.2. MONITORING YOUR DOG'S HEALTH DURING TRANSITION

As you introduce new foods, you must watch for signs of how well your dog adapts. Monitor their energy levels, appetite, weight, and behavior. Changes in stool consistency, excessive gas, or signs of discomfort should be noted, as these might indicate how well your dog is adjusting to the new diet.

Regular check-ins with your vet can be immensely helpful, providing professional insights and reassurance throughout the transition phase.

Keeping a journal can also be beneficial to track what works and what doesn't, ensuring that you're on the right path to optimizing your dog's health through diet.

A healthy transition should see your dog thriving, with a shiny coat and a good energy level. If you notice any digestive upsets or lethargy or their coat loses its luster, it might be time to adjust the proportions or ingredients.

2.3. ADDITIONAL TIPS FOR IMPLEMENTING THE TRANSITION SCHEDULE

Prepare in Advance: Before starting the transition, prepare balanced homemade recipes for your dog's nutritional needs.

Measure Accurately: Use a kitchen scale or measuring cups to ensure that commercial and homemade food proportions are accurate according to the transition schedule.

Adjust as Needed: If your dog shows signs of gastrointestinal distress, slow the transition by sticking to the current mix for a couple more days before proceeding.

Hydration is Key: Ensure your dog remains well-hydrated throughout the transition. Changing diets can affect hydration levels.

Final Check-Up: Once your dog has fully transitioned to homemade food, consider a veterinary check-up to ensure it is in good health and meeting its dietary needs.

2.4. AVOIDING COMMON MISTAKES

One common mistake is changing the diet too quickly or introducing too many new ingredients at a time. It can overwhelm your dog's digestive system.

Another error is neglecting the balance of nutrients — homemade food must be more than just tasty; it needs to be nutritionally complete, which means it should include the right proportions of proteins, fats, carbohydrates, vitamins, and minerals.

Also, be wary of the temptation to feed your pet human food that may be harmful to dogs, such as onions, chocolate, grapes, or certain nuts. Chapter 3 of this book lists foods your dog should avoid.

Finally, avoid overly rich or spicy foods that could cause stomach upset. Also, avoid overly relying on supplements without understanding their necessity and proper dosage, which could lead to nutrient imbalances.

Educating yourself on canine nutrition and planning meals can help you avoid these pitfalls.

2.5. TOOLS AND EQUIPMENT FOR FOOD PREPARATION

Preparing your dog's food at home doesn't require sophisticated gadgets, but a few essential tools can make the process easier and more efficient. Here's what you'll find handy:

- Quality knives and durable cutting board: for chopping vegetables and meats.
- Measuring cups and spoons: to ensure accurate nutrient proportions.
- Blender or food processor: for making purees or mixing ingredients.
- Large mixing bowls: for combining ingredients before cooking.
- Slow cooker or pressure cooker: perfect for making stews and cooking meat thoroughly.
- Airtight storage containers: for storing prepared food. They will keep it fresh and ready to serve for several days, simplifying your daily routine.

Transitioning to homemade dog food can be challenging, but with careful planning, observation, and a touch of culinary love, it can be a gratifying endeavor that enriches your dog's life.

Having the right tools is essential to creating good meals for your dog. With careful planning, attentive monitoring, and the right tools, you'll be well-equipped to provide your dog with nutritious, delicious meals tailored just for them.

CHAPTER 3

SAFE FEEDING TIPS

3.1. LIST OF SAFE FOODS FOR DOGS

As dog owners increasingly look to enrich their pets' diets with healthy, human-grade foods, understanding a broader range of safe options can help craft enjoyable and nutritious meals. This section builds upon the essential list of safe foods for dogs, introducing more diverse choices that can benefit your dog's diet, all while keeping safety and dietary needs in mind.

3.1.1. Safe Fruits and Vegetables

Fruits

- Apples — Rich in vitamins A and C, apples are great for your dog, but always remove the seeds and core first.
- Bananas — High in potassium and fiber, bananas are an excellent occasional treat. However, due to their sugar content, they should be given sparingly.
- Blueberries — Known for their antioxidant properties, blueberries are beneficial for dogs, supporting cell health and providing fiber.
- Cantaloupe — This melon is safe for dogs and a good source of vitamins A and C, but due to its sugar content, it should be offered in moderation.
- Watermelon — Free from seeds and rind, watermelon is hydrating and full of vitamins A, B6, and C.
- Pears — High in fiber and vitamins C and K, pears can be a healthy dog snack when the seeds and pit are removed.
- Peaches — Good for a dog's skin and coat health, peaches are nutritious but must be offered without the pit.
- Mango — This tropical fruit is packed with vitamins A, B6, C, and E but should be served without the pit.
- Strawberries — Full of fiber and vitamin C, strawberries can be a sweet treat in moderation due to their sugar content.
- Raspberries — Low in sugar and high in fiber, vitamins, and antioxidants, raspberries are great in small amounts, especially for aging dogs.

Vegetables

- Carrots — Both raw and cooked carrots are nutritious for dogs, offering fiber and vitamin A. They can also help clean teeth naturally.
- Green Beans and Peas - Plain green and peas beans are a healthy, low-calorie dog snack that provides iron and vitamins.
- Pumpkin — Cooked pumpkin is an excellent source of fiber and beta-carotene.
- Sweet Potatoes - Cooked sweet potatoes are rich in fiber, vitamin B6, vitamin C, and beta-carotene.
- Spinach — Although high in vitamins A, B, C, and K, spinach should be fed in small quantities due to its oxalic acid content.
- Brussels Sprouts Are rich in nutrients and antioxidants, but they should be given in moderation due to their potential to cause gas.
- Cucumbers — Great for overweight dogs, cucumbers contain little to no carbohydrates, fats, or oils and can boost energy levels.

- Celery — Known to freshen dog breath and be rich in vitamins A, B, and C, celery should be cut into small, chewable pieces to avoid choking dogs.
- Broccoli — Rich in fiber and vitamin C, broccoli is safe in minimal quantities, as it can cause gastric irritation in some dogs.
- Zucchini — Safe and healthy, zucchini is low in calories and a good source of vitamin C.

3.1.2. Safe Proteins

Meats

- Chicken — Cooked, boneless, and skinless chicken is an excellent source of protein for dogs and is often used as a meal replacement ingredient.
- Turkey — Like chicken, cooked turkey is safe but should be served plain and boneless. Avoid turkey skin, which contains high fats.
- Beef — Plain-cooked beef provides iron and protein.
- Lean Pork — Cooked plain pork without any spices or additives can be a good protein source, but it should be given occasionally due to its higher fat content.
- Lamb — Often used in dog food for pets with allergies, cooked lamb is another excellent protein source.

Dairy and Eggs

- Eggs — Fully cooked eggs can be a great source of protein. Ensure they are cooked without oil or butter.
- Cottage Cheese — Low in fat and high in calcium, cottage cheese is a suitable occasional treat for dogs.
- Plain Yogurt — High in calcium and protein, plain yogurt is suitable for a dog's digestive system, provided it contains no added sugars or artificial sweeteners.
- Hard Cheese — In small amounts, hard cheeses like cheddar can be a good source of protein and calcium.

By incorporating a wider variety of safe fruits, vegetables, proteins, and grains into a dog's diet, you can provide them with enhanced nutrition and improved health benefits. Remember to keep all new introductions moderate and balanced to maintain overall dietary health and prioritize your dog's specific nutritional needs. This approach ensures your pet enjoys a healthy, happy, and vibrant life.

Always consider the advice of a vet, especially when making significant changes to your dog's diet or when dealing with health issues.

3.2. List of Toxic and Harmful Foods for Dogs to Avoid

Understanding what foods harm dogs is as important as knowing what is safe. This knowledge helps prevent accidental poisoning and health complications, ensuring a safer environment for your pet. This section outlines common foods that should be avoided in a dog's diet, detailing why they are harmful and their potential health risks.

Daily Food Intake Table

Food Item	Why It's Harmful	Severity
Chocolate	Contains theobromine and caffeine, toxic to dogs and can lead to vomiting, diarrhea, rapid heart rate, seizures, and even death	Highly toxic, even in small amounts
Grapes and Raisins	Can cause acute kidney failure in dogs. The exact toxic substance is unknown, but the effects are severe	Very dangerous, even in small quantities
Grapes and Raisins	Can cause acute kidney failure in dogs. The exact toxic substance is unknown, but the effects are severe	Very dangerous, even in small quantities
Onions and Garlic	Contain thiosulfate, which causes oxidative damage to red blood cells, leading to anemia. Includes all forms (raw, cooked, powder)	Toxic in moderate to large quantities
Xylitol	A sugar substitute found in many products, including gum, candy, and some peanut butters. Causes rapid insulin release, resulting in hypoglycemia and potential liver failure	Extremely toxic; small amounts can be fatal
Alcohol	Even small amounts in beverages, syrups, or food can be dangerous. Causes vomiting, diarrhea, central nervous system depression, difficulty breathing, coma, and death	Highly toxic
Caffeine	Found in coffee, tea, soda, and energy drinks; can be fatal. Symptoms include rapid breathing, heart palpitations, and muscle tremors	Highly toxic, similar to chocolate
Macadamia Nuts	Can cause weakness, depression, vomiting, tremors, and hyperthermia in dogs	Toxic; symptoms can occur with as little as six nuts

Avocado	Contains persin, causing vomiting and diarrhea. The pit also poses a choking hazard and can obstruct the gastrointestinal tract	Mild to moderate toxicity
Yeast Dough	Can rise and cause gas accumulation in the digestive system, potentially causing rupture of the stomach or intestines	Potentially life-threatening if a large amount is ingested
Bones	Cooked bones can splinter and cause obstruction or lacerations in the digestive system	Severity can vary; emergencies in case of serious injuries or obstructions

Extended Table of toxic Foods for Dogs

This expanded table delves deeper into the list of foods toxic to dogs, including some that might not be as widely recognized. Understanding these dangers can help prevent accidental ingestions that could lead to serious health complications or even fatal outcomes.

Food Item	Why It's Harmful	Severity
Persimmons, Peaches, and Plums	The seeds or pits can cause intestinal obstruction or enteritis, and the pits contain cyanide, which is toxic	Moderate to severe, varies by amount and dog siz.
Salt	Excessive intake can lead to sodium ion poisoning, causing vomiting, diarrhea, tremors, and seizures, potentially leading to death	Moderate to severe, depends on amount ingested
Nutmeg	Contains myristicin, which can cause seizures and central nervous system problems	Can be severe if consumed in large quantities
Raw Eggs	May contain salmonella and decrease the absorption of biotin, leading to skin and coat problems	Generally moderate; concerns for bacterial infection
Raw Meat and Fish*	Can contain bacteria causing food poisoning. Certain fish can carry parasites causing fatal "salmon poisoning disease"	Varies from mild to severe, based on the source
Fat Trimmings and Bones	Fat can cause pancreatitis; bones can splinter and cause obstruction or lacerations of the digestive system	Moderate to severe; bones can cause life-threatening injuries

Citrus	Stems, leaves, peels, fruit, and seeds contain citric acid and essential oils, causing irritation and possible CNS depression	Mild to moderate for fruit; severe for other parts
Milk and Dairy Products**	Dogs are often lactose intolerant, leading to diarrhea and digestive upset.	Generally mild but discomforting
Coconut and Coconut Oil	Can cause stomach upset and diarrhea. Coconut water is high in potassium and not recommended for dog.	Mild to moderate.
Human Vitamins Containing Iron	Iron can damage the digestive lining and be toxic to the liver and kidneys	Moderate to severe, depending on the amount ingested

*Read more about raw meat in the diet of dogs in Section 3.3.
**Foods made from fermented milk, such as yogurt and cottage cheese, generally do not cause negative reactions when consumed in moderation

By keeping these lists of toxic foods in mind, you can protect your dog from any common hazards, contributing to a longer, healthier life for your companion.

Preventative Measures

- Ensure all family members and visitors know which foods are unsafe for dogs to prevent accidental ingestion.
- Keep all potentially toxic foods securely stored away from where dogs can access them.
- If your dog consumes any of these toxic foods, it is crucial to seek vet care immediately.
- Regular vet visits help keep track of your pet's health and preempt any diet-related issues.

By staying informed and vigilant, dog owners can significantly reduce the risk of their pets ingesting harmful substances, thus ensuring their health, happiness, and longevity.

3.3. RAW MEAT IN THE DIET OF DOGS. PROS AND CONS

Feeding raw meat to dogs is a contentious topic among veterinarians, pet experts, and pet owners alike. Here are the detailed arguments for and against this feeding approach:

Arguments in Favor of Raw Meat Diets:

- Natural Diet Alignment. Proponents of raw feeding argue that this diet is closer to the natural eating habits of dogs' wild ancestors and includes more natural ingredients, which they believe are more biologically appropriate for dogs.

- Improved Coat and Skin Health. Many owners report that their dogs' coats become shinier and their skin healthier after switching to a raw meat diet. This is often attributed to raw meat's natural fats and oils, which are not always as prevalent in cooked or processed dog foods.
- Dental Health Benefits. Chewing raw, meaty bones can help reduce plaque and tartar build-up on dogs' teeth, potentially leading to better overall dental health and less gum disease.
- Increased Energy and Overall Health Improvement. Some pet owners observe an increase in their dog's energy levels and an improvement in their overall health and vitality when fed a raw diet. These changes are often linked to the high-quality protein and nutrients naturally present in uncooked meat.

Arguments Against Raw Meat Diets:

- Health Risks. Raw meat can harbor pathogens such as Salmonella, E. coli, and Listeria, which pose health risks to the dogs and humans handling the raw food. These bacteria can cause severe gastrointestinal illnesses and other health complications.
- Nutritional Imbalances. A raw meat diet can lead to dietary deficiencies or excesses if not carefully balanced. Essential vitamins, minerals, and other nutrients must be carefully managed to ensure the diet meets a dog's nutritional needs, which can be particularly challenging with homemade raw diets.
- Complexity in Diet Preparation. Properly preparing and balancing a raw diet requires significant knowledge and effort from the dog owner. It involves understanding dogs' nutritional needs and how to meet them with various raw ingredients, which can be daunting for many pet owners.
- Higher Cost. Raw meat diets are often more expensive than commercial dog foods. The cost of purchasing high-quality raw meat, bones, and supplements can be financially burdensome over time, making this feeding option less accessible to some pet owners.

Recommendations: Before transitioning to a raw meat diet, it is crucial to consult with a veterinarian who can assess whether this diet is suitable for your dog and help you balance it properly to avoid nutritional deficiencies. Additionally, strict hygiene practices should be adhered to when preparing and storing raw meat to minimize health risks. This includes washing hands and surfaces thoroughly and keeping raw meat separate from other foods to prevent cross-contamination.

3.4. SIGNS OF NUTRIENT IMBALANCE

Feeding your dog homemade food can be highly rewarding and offer a tailored diet to meet their specific health needs. Ensuring your dog receives a balanced diet is crucial, as nutrient imbalances can lead to various health issues. Recognizing the signs of nutrient imbalances is vital for maintaining your dog's health. This section will discuss critical indicators suggesting a nutrient imbalance in your dog's diet.

Critical Signs of Nutrient Imbalance

Sign	Description	Nutrients Often Involved
Poor Coat Quality	A healthy dog should have a shiny, smooth coat. If a dog's diet lacks essential fatty acids or the right balance of nutrients, the coat may become dull, brittle, or excessively oily	Omega-3 and omega-6 fatty acids, zinc, vitamins A and E
Skin Issues	Nutrient deficiencies can lead to dry, flaky, or itchy skin, and in some cases, can cause hair loss or excessive scratching, which can lead to infections	Vitamins A, E, B vitamins, zinc, essential fatty acids
Digestive Problems	Imbalances often manifest as diarrhea, constipation, or vomiting. These symptoms can stem from deficiencies or excesses in specific nutrients, such as fiber, proteins, and certain minerals	Dietary fiber, protein, calcium
Weight Loss or Gain	Unexpected weight changes can be a sign of nutrient imbalances. Excessive weight gain might indicate too many calories or a lack of exercise, whereas weight loss might suggest a deficiency in calories or essential nutrients	Overall calorie intake, protein, carbohydrates
Low Energy Levels	A lack of essential nutrients, particularly B vitamins, iron, or protein, can lead to decreased energy levels and lethargy	B vitamins, iron, protein
Dental and Bone Problems	Poor nutrition can contribute to bad breath, weak or broken teeth, and gum disease. Calcium and phosphorus ratios are particularly important for maintaining dental health	Calcium, phosphorus, vitamin D
Muscle Tone and Strength	Muscle weakness and difficulty recovering from normal activity	Essential amino acids, proteins, fats, calcium and phosphorus
Behavioral Changes	Nutritional deficiencies can affect a dog's behavior. Signs include anxiety, irritability, or a sudden change in behavior, such as increased aggression	Magnesium, zinc, omega-3 fatty acids

Please be sure to observe your dog. Pay close attention to your dog's physical condition and behavior; changes can be subtle but indicate a more significant issue.

A well-balanced diet is crucial for maintaining your dog's health and preventing nutrient imbalances. By being aware of the signs of nutrient deficiencies and excesses, you can take proactive steps to adjust your dog's diet as needed. Always involve a veterinary professional when making significant changes to ensure your dog receives all the necessary nutrients for a healthy life.

3.5. IDENTIFYING POTENTIAL ALLERGENS

When preparing homemade meals for your dog, it is crucial to identify and understand potential allergens that could affect your pet's health. This section will help you recognize common allergens, observe signs of allergic reactions, and provide first-aid measures.

3.5.1. Types of Common Allergens

- *Proteins*: Protein sources, particularly beef, chicken, eggs, and dairy, are the most common allergens in dog food.
- *Fish and lamb* can also sometimes trigger allergies.
- *Grains*: Some dogs can be allergic to grains like wheat, corn, and soy or the gluten found in certain grains.
- *Additives and Preservatives*: Chemicals added to enhance flavor, color, or shelf life can trigger allergies. These include, but are not limited to, BHA, BHT, ethoxyquin, and artificial colorings. When preparing homemade food, it is easier to avoid these additives, but be mindful of any unusual ingredients you might introduce.
- *Environmental Allergens*: Pollen, molds, and dust can also trigger allergies, though they are less about food and more about the environment. They can contaminate food storage areas.

3.5.2. Signs of Allergic Reactions

Be on the lookout for the following symptoms which may indicate that your dog is having an allergic reaction to something in their diet:

- *Skin Irritations*: Redness, hives, itchy rashes, or swelling, particularly around the face, ears, paws, and underbelly.
- *Gastrointestinal Issues*: Diarrhea, vomiting, and excessive gas are common signs of food allergies.
- *Ear Infections*: Persistent ear infections can indicate a food allergy, especially if they recur even after treatment.
- *Chronic Itching and Scratching*: If your dog constantly scratches or bites at their skin or rubs their body against furniture, it might be due to discomfort caused by allergies
- *Respiratory Distress*: Although less common, some dogs might exhibit coughing, sneezing, or wheezing.

3.5.3. First Aid for Allergic Reactions

If you suspect your dog is experiencing an allergic reaction, take the following steps:

- Remove the Suspected Allergen: If you suspect a food-related allergy, stop feeding your dog the new ingredient and revert to their previous diet.
- Soothing Baths: Soothing oatmeal baths can relieve discomfort from skin irritations. Please ensure that any shampoo or soap used is hypoallergenic and free of colorants and perfumes.
- Cool Compresses: For localized skin reactions, applying a cool compress can help relieve itching and swelling.
- Medications: Over-the-counter antihistamines can sometimes be used for immediate relief from mild allergy symptoms, but always consult your vet before administering any medication to determine the correct dosage.
- Emergency Care: If your dog shows signs of severe distress, such as difficulty breathing or extreme swelling, seek emergency veterinary care immediately. This can be indicative of anaphylaxis, a life-threatening reaction. Your vet may prescribe stronger medications or recommend allergy testing to identify specific allergens.

3.5.4. Monitoring and Management

Once you identify that your dog has a food allergy, it is important to monitor its diet carefully. A detailed food diary can help you track ingredients and correlate them with any allergic reactions. Work closely with your veterinarian to develop a feeding plan that avoids known allergens and still provides the nutritional balance your dog needs.

By paying attention to the signs of allergies and knowing how to respond, you can ensure that your homemade dog food not only keeps your pet happy and healthy but also safe from potential allergens.

CHAPTER 4

MAIN DISHES RECIPES

4.1. RED MEAT DISHES

4.1.1. Why Red Meat Should Be a Staple in Your Dog's Bowl

• *Packed with Goodness*: Who knew that red meat could be so important? It's a fantastic source of high-quality protein that helps keep your dog's muscles strong and ready for play. Plus, it's loaded with B vitamins, especially vitamin B12, a superstar for keeping nerves healthy and energy levels high.

• *Healthy Fats and Essential Minerals*: Red meat doesn't just taste great; it is full of good fats that keep your dog's coat shiny and skin healthy. And let's not forget about the minerals like iron, zinc, and selenium. These aren't just fancy words—they help boost your pup's immune system and keep their thyroid in check.

• *They Just Love It*: Let's face it, dogs go nuts for red meat. It's a taste they love naturally, making mealtime fun and nourishing. Incorporating red meat into your dog's homemade meals can increase their enthusiasm for mealtime, ensuring they receive the necessary nutrients without fuss. Seeing your furry friend happy and healthy is what it's all about, right?

• *Mix Things Up*: While red meat is awesome, variety is the spice of life—or, in this case, the spice of your dog's diet. Mix in other proteins like chicken, fish, and even some veggies to keep meals interesting and nutritionally balanced.

• *Just Right for Your Dog*: Remember, every dog is unique. Some might need less red meat for health reasons like kidney conditions or allergies. It's always best to chat with your vet to make sure you're giving your dog the best possible diet tailored just for them.

By tossing some red meat into your dog's homemade meals, you're not just filling their bowl - you're filling it with love and essential nutrients. Just like us, dogs deserve a delicious and healthy diet, and with your homemade meals, they'll get just that!

4.1.2. Red Meat Dishes Recipes

The following pages contain plenty of healthy and delicious red meat recipes for your furry friend. Try them and treat your dog to something special today!

SIMPLE BEEF STEW

Cubes of beef cooked slowly with carrots and peas in a beef broth

Protein: 50% | Fat: 30% | Carbohydrates: 15% | Minerals and vitamins: 5%

1 h 30 min	48 oz	960 (20 per oz) kcal

INGREDIENTS

- 1.5 lbs lean beef, cut into small cubes
- 4 medium carrots, peeled and diced
- 1 cup peas (fresh or frozen)
- 4 cups low-sodium beef broth
- 1 tbsp olive oil
- Water (if needed)

DIRECTIONS

1. **Prep:** Heat the olive oil in a large pot over medium heat. Add the beef cubes and sear until all sides are browned, about 5-7 minutes.
2. **Simmer:** Add the diced carrots and the beef broth to the pot. Bring the mixture to a boil, then reduce the heat to a low simmer. Cover and let it cook for about 1 hour or until the beef is tender.
3. **Add Peas:** After the beef and carrots are cooked, add the peas to the pot. Cook for an additional 10 minutes. If the stew seems too thick, add some water to achieve the desired consistency.
4. **Cool Down:** Remove the stew from heat and let it cool to room temperature before serving to avoid burning your dog's mouth.

BEEF PATTY BAKE

Ground beef patties baked until fully cooked; serve with a side of mashed pumpkin

Protein: 60% | Fat: 25% | Carbohydrates: 10% | Minerals and vitamins: 5%

1 h 30 min	48 oz	1200 (25 per oz) kcal

INGREDIENTS

- 2 lbs lean ground beef
- 2 cups pumpkin puree (fresh or canned, but ensure it's unsweetened and unseasoned)
- 1 tsp of olive oil
- A pinch of salt (optional)

DIRECTIONS

1. **Preheat Oven:** Preheat your oven to 375°F (190°C).
2. **Form Patties:** Divide the ground beef into equal portions and form into patties. The size of the patties can be adjusted.
3. **Prep Baking Sheet:** Lightly grease a baking sheet with olive oil.
4. **Bake Patties:** Place the patties on the baking sheet and bake for 25-30 minutes, ensuring the meat is fully cooked.
5. **Prep Mashed Pumpkin:** While the patties are baking, heat the pumpkin puree in a small saucepan over medium heat. You can add a little water to achieve a smoother consistency. Heat through for about 5-10 minutes, stirring occasionally.
6. **Cool and Serve:** Allow the patties and pumpkin to cool to room temperature before serving to your dog to prevent burns.

PORK AND SPINACH MINI ROLLS

Minced pork rolled with spinach in small, bite-sized pieces

Protein: 55% | Fat: 35% | Carbohydrates: 5% | Minerals and vitamins: 5%

40 min	48 oz	1200 (25 per oz) kcal

INGREDIENTS

- 2 lbs lean minced pork
- 2 cups fresh spinach, finely chopped
- 1 tbsp olive oil
- Water, as needed

DIRECTIONS

1. **Preheat the Oven:** Set your oven to 375°F (190°C).
2. **Prep the Filling:** In a large bowl, mix the minced pork with finely chopped spinach. Distribute the spinach evenly through the pork.
3. **Form the Rolls:** Take small amounts of the pork-spinach mixture and form them into small, elongated rolls.
4. **Cooking Setup:** Line a baking tray with parchment paper and lightly brush it with olive oil to prevent sticking. Arrange the mini rolls on the tray, ensuring they do not touch each other.
5. **Bake:** Place the tray in the oven and bake for 25-30 minutes or until the rolls are golden brown and fully cooked.
6. **Cool Down:** Allow the rolls to cool completely before serving to your dog to ensure they are safe to eat.

LIVER AND APPLE BITES

Chopped liver (pork or beef) mixed with grated apple and baked into small treats

Protein: 60% | Fat: 25% | Carbohydrates: 10% | Minerals and vitamins: 5%

40 min	36 oz	900 (25 per oz) kcal

INGREDIENTS

- 1 lb liver (pork or beef), finely chopped
- 2 medium apples, cored and grated (ensure they are free from seeds)
- 1 egg (to help bind the ingredients)
- 1 tbsp olive oil (for greasing the baking tray)

DIRECTIONS

1. **Preheat Oven:** Set your oven to 350°F (175°C).
2. **Prep the Mixture:** In a large mixing bowl, combine the finely chopped liver, grated apples, and egg. Mix well until all the ingredients are evenly distributed.
3. **Prep the Baking Tray:** Grease a baking sheet with olive oil to prevent sticking.
4. **Shape the Treats:** Scoop small portions of the liver and apple mixture and shape them into bite-sized balls. Place them onto the baking tray.
5. **Bake:** Put the baking sheet in the oven and bake for 25-30 minutes until the treats are firm and slightly browned on the outside.
6. **Cooling:** Allow the treats to cool completely on a rack before serving to ensure they are safe for your dog to eat.

BISON BITES

Small chunks of bison meat simmered with sweet potato cubes

Protein: 55% | Fat: 25% | Carbohydrates: 15% | Minerals and vitamins: 5%

1 h	40 oz	800 (20 per oz) kcal

INGREDIENTS

- 1.5 lbs of bison meat, cut into small chunks
- 2 large sweet potatoes, peeled and cubed
- 4 cups low-sodium beef or vegetable broth
- 1 tbsp olive oil

DIRECTIONS

1. **Prep:** Heat the olive oil in a large pot over medium heat.
2. **Brown the Bison:** Add the bison chunks to the pot and brown them evenly. This should take about 5-7 minutes.
3. **Add Sweet Potatoes:** Once the bison is browned, add the cubed sweet potatoes to the pot.
4. **Add Broth and Simmer:** Pour the broth over the mixture. Bring it to a boil, then reduce the heat and let it simmer covered for about 45 minutes until the sweet potatoes are soft and the bison is tender.
5. **Cool Before Serving:** Let the dish cool to room temperature to ensure it's safe for your dog to eat.

MEATLOAF MINIS

Mini meatloaves made with ground beef, oats, and finely chopped celery

Protein: 45% | Fat: 35% | Carbohydrates: 15% | Minerals and vitamins: 5%

50 min	48 oz	1200 (25 per oz) kcal

INGREDIENTS

- 2 lbs ground beef
- 1 cup rolled oats
- 1 cup finely chopped celery
- 2 eggs
- 1/2 cup low-sodium beef broth
- 2 tbsps flaxseed meal (optional, for added fiber and omega-3 fatty acids)

DIRECTIONS

1. **Preheat Oven:** Set your oven to 350°F (175°C).
2. **Mix Ingredients:** In a large mixing bowl, combine the ground beef, rolled oats, chopped celery, eggs, beef broth, and flaxseed meal. Mix thoroughly until all ingredients are evenly distributed.
3. **Form Mini Meatloaves:** Shape the mixture into small, individual meatloaf portions about the size of a golf ball or slightly larger, depending on your dog's size. Place them on a greased baking sheet.
4. **Bake:** Bake in the preheated oven for about 40 minutes, or until the meatloaves are cooked through and the tops are slightly browned.
5. **Cool Before Serving:** Allow the mini meatloaves to cool completely before serving to ensure they are safe for your dog to eat.

GROUND LAMB AND RICE

Ground lamb cooked with brown rice and chopped carrots

Protein: 40% | Fat: 30% | Carbohydrates: 25% | Minerals and vitamins: 5%

⏱ 1 h	🍲 48 oz	🍽 960 (20 per oz) kcal

INGREDIENTS

- 1.5 lbs ground lamb
- 2 cups brown rice
- 2 large carrots, peeled and finely chopped
- 4 cups water or low-sodium vegetable broth
- 1 tbsp olive oil

DIRECTIONS

1. **Prep the Rice:** Rinse the rice under cold water until the water runs clear to remove excess starch and improve digestibility.
2. **Cook the Rice:** Combine the rice, water, or broth in a large pot and boil. Reduce the heat to low, cover, and simmer for about 45 minutes.
3. **Cook the Lamb:** While the rice is cooking, heat the olive oil in a skillet over medium heat. Add the ground lamb and cook until it's browned and fully cooked, breaking it apart with a spoon as it cooks.
4. **Add Carrots:** Add the finely chopped carrots to the skillet. Cook together for an additional 10 minutes until the carrots are soft.
5. **Combine Ingredients:** Combine the rice and the lamb in a large pot. Stir well to mix all the ingredients thoroughly.
6. **Cool Before Serving:** Let it cool to ensure it's safe for your dog to eat.

LIVER AND PEA PILAF

Beef liver cooked with peas and brown rice, seasoned lightly

Protein: 50% | Fat: 30% | Carbohydrates: 15% | Minerals and vitamins: 5%

⏱ 1 h	🍲 48 oz	🍽 1200 (25 per oz) kcal

INGREDIENTS

- 1 lb beef liver, finely chopped
- 1.5 cups brown rice
- 1 cup peas (fresh or frozen)
- 4 cups water
- 1 tbsp olive oil

DIRECTIONS

1. **Prep Rice:** Rinsing the brown rice thoroughly under cold water until the water runs clear to remove any excess starch.
2. **Cook Rice:** Add the rice and 4 cups of water to a large pot. Bring to a boil, then reduce to a simmer, cover, and cook for about 45 minutes.
3. **Cook Liver:** Heat the olive oil in a skillet over medium heat. Add the chopped liver and cook until fully cooked, about 10 minutes.
4. **Add Peas:** Add the peas to the skillet. If using frozen peas, allow them to thaw slightly before adding them. Cook together for 5 minutes.
5. **Combine Ingredients:** When both are ready, combine the rice and liver mixture in the pot. Mix well to integrate all the ingredients.
6. **Cool Before Serving:** Allow the pilaf to cool to room temperature before serving to ensure it is safe for your dog to eat.

BEEFY ZUCCHINI SLICES

Thin slices of beef cooked alongside zucchini strips

Protein: 60% | Fat: 25% | Carbohydrates: 10% | Minerals and vitamins: 5%

| 🕐 30 min | 40 oz | 800 (20 per oz) kcal |

INGREDIENTS

- 1.5 lbs lean beef, thinly sliced
- 2 large zucchinis, cut into thin strips
- 1 tbsp olive oil

DIRECTIONS

1. **Preheat Skillet:** Heat the olive oil in a large skillet over medium-high heat.
2. **Cook the Beef:** Add the thinly sliced beef to the skillet. Cook for 2-3 minutes on each side or until the beef is browned and cooked. Remove from the skillet and set aside.
3. **Cook the Zucchini:** Add the zucchini strips to the same skillet. Cook for about 5-7 minutes, stirring occasionally, until the zucchini is tender but still crisp.
4. **Combine Ingredients:** Return the beef slices to the skillet with the zucchini, toss together, and heat through for 2 minutes.
5. **Cool Before Serving:** Let the dish cool to room temperature before serving to ensure it's safe for your dog.

SIMPLE GROUND VENISON

Ground venison served with rice

Protein: 55% | Fat: 30% | Carbohydrates: 10% | Minerals and vitamins: 5%

| 🕐 45 min | 48 oz | 960 (20 per oz) kcal |

INGREDIENTS

- 1.5 lbs ground venison
- 1.5 cups brown rice
- 4 cups water
- 1 tbsp olive oil

DIRECTIONS

1. **Cook Rice:** Rinse the rice under cold water until the water runs clear. Combine the rice and 4 cups of water in a medium pot. Bring to a boil, then reduce to a simmer, cover, and cook for 35-40 minutes, or until the water is absorbed.
2. **Cook Venison:** Heat the olive oil in a large skillet over medium heat. Add the ground venison. Cook, stirring frequently to break up the meat, until the venison is fully cooked, about 10 minutes.
3. **Combine Ingredients:** Mix the rice and venison together in a large bowl or pot. Stir well to combine.
4. **Cool Before Serving:** Allow the mixture to cool to room temperature before serving to ensure it's safe for your dog.

PORK AND CUCUMBER COOL DOWN

Thinly sliced pork served with chilled cucumbers and a dab of plain yogurt

Protein: 50% | Fat: 30% | Carbohydrates: 15% | Minerals and vitamins: 5%

20 min	40 oz	800 (20 per oz) kcal

INGREDIENTS

- 1.5 lbs lean pork, thinly sliced
- 2 large cucumbers, peeled and thinly sliced
- 1/2 cup plain yogurt (ensure it's unsweetened and unflavored)
- 1 tbsp olive oil

DIRECTIONS

1. **Cook Pork:** Heat the olive oil in a skillet over medium heat. Add the thinly sliced pork and cook until it's entirely done and slightly browned, about 10-12 minutes. Stir occasionally to ensure even cooking.
2. **Prep Cucumbers:** Peel and thinly slice the cucumbers while cooking pork. Place them in the refrigerator to chill.
3. **Combine and Serve:** Once the pork is cooked and cooled to room temperature, mix the sliced pork with the chilled cucumber slices. Before serving, top each serving with a tablespoon of plain yogurt.

LIVER VEGETABLE MEDLEY

Mixed liver (pork and beef) sautéed with zucchini and bell peppers

Protein: 55% | Fat: 25% | Carbohydrates: 15% | Minerals and vitamins: 5%

30 min	48 oz	1200 (25 per oz) kcal

INGREDIENTS

- 1 lb beef liver)
- 1 lb pork liver
- 2 medium zucchinis, sliced
- 2 bell peppers (one red, one yellow), seeded and sliced
- 1 tbsp olive oil

DIRECTIONS

1. **Prep Ingredients:** Slice the beef and pork liver into thin strips. Wash and slice the zucchini and bell peppers.
2. **Heat Oil:** Heat the olive oil over medium heat in a large skillet.
3. **Cook Liver:** Add the liver strips to the skillet and sauté until they start to brown, about 5-7 minutes. Be careful not to overcook it.
4. **Add Vegetables:** Add the sliced zucchini and bell peppers to the skillet with the liver. Continue to sauté until the vegetables are tender but still crisp, about another 5-7 minutes.
5. **Cool Before Serving:** Allow the dish to cool to room temperature before serving to ensure it's safe for your dog.

GROUND BEEF AND CARROT SOUP

Ground beef simmered with carrots, celery, and a touch of turmeric

Protein:45% | Fat: 35% | Carbohydrates: 15% | Minerals and vitamins: 5%

50 min	64 oz	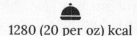 1280 (20 per oz) kcal

INGREDIENTS

- 2 lbs ground beef
- 4 large carrots, peeled and diced
- 2 stalks celery, diced
- 1 tsp turmeric powder
- 6 cups water or low-sodium beef broth
- 1 tbsp olive oil

DIRECTIONS

1. **Prep Ingredients:** Peel and dice the carrots and celery into bite-sized pieces. Measure out the turmeric powder.
2. **Brown the Beef:** Heat the olive oil in a large pot over medium heat.
3. **Add the ground beef** and cook, breaking it into small pieces as it cooks.
4. **Add Vegetables:** Add the diced carrots and celery to the pot, stirring to combine.
5. **Season:** Sprinkle the turmeric over the meat and vegetables, mixing well to distribute the spice evenly.
6. **Simmer:** Pour in the water or beef broth, bringing the mixture to a boil. Reduce the heat to low and let it simmer for about 30 minutes, or until the vegetables are tender.
7. **Cool Before Serving:** Allow the soup to cool to room temperature before serving to ensure it's safe for your dog.

SIMPLE VENISON STRIPS

Strips of venison cooked quickly in a pan and served with boiled peas

Protein: 60% | Fat: 25% | Carbohydrates: 10% | Minerals and vitamins: 5%

25 min	40 oz	1000 (25 per oz) kcal

INGREDIENTS

- 2 lbs venison, cut into thin strips
- 1 cup peas (fresh or frozen)
- 1 tbsp olive oil
- Water for boiling peas

DIRECTIONS

1. **Prep Ingredients:** Trim any excess fat from the venison and cut it into thin strips suitable for quick cooking. Measure out the peas.
2. **Cook Venison:** Heat the olive oil in a large skillet over medium-high heat. Add the venison strips and cook for 5-7 minutes, stirring occasionally.
3. **Boil Peas:** Bring a small pot of water to a boil. Add the peas and cook for 5 minutes or until tender. Drain the peas once cooked.
4. **Combine and Serve:** Once the venison and peas are cooked, mix them in a serving dish.
5. **Cool Before Serving:** Allow the dish to cool to room temperature to ensure it's safe for your dog.

BISON AND BEET CUBES

Cubes of bison meat cooked with diced beets

Protein: 55% | Fat: 30% | Carbohydrates: 10% | Minerals and vitamins: 5%

40 min	48 oz	1200 (25 per oz) kcal

INGREDIENTS

- 2 lbs bison meat, cut into small cubes
- 2 large beets, peeled and diced
- 1 tbsp coconut oil (for cooking)
- Water (as needed for cooking)

DIRECTIONS

1. **Prep Ingredients**: Peel and dice the beets. Cube the bison meat into bite-sized pieces.
2. **Cook Bison**: Heat the coconut oil in a large skillet over medium heat. Add the bison cubes and cook until browned on all sides, 7-10 minutes.
3. **Add Beets**: Add the diced beets to the skillet with the bison. Stir to combine.
4. **Simmer**: Add a small amount of water to the skillet (just enough to cover the bottom), reduce the heat to low, cover, and let simmer for 20-25 minutes, or until the beets are tender and the bison is fully cooked.
5. **Cool Before Serving**: Allow the dish to cool to room temperature to ensure it's safe for your dog.

BEEF AND EGG SCRAMBLE

Scrambled ground beef with eggs and finely chopped broccoli

Protein: 60% | Fat: 30% | Carbohydrates: 5% | Minerals and vitamins: 5%

25 min	40 oz	1200 (30 per oz) kcal

INGREDIENTS

- 1.5 lbs ground beef
- 4 large eggs
- 1 cup finely chopped broccoli
- 1 tbsp olive oil

DIRECTIONS

1. **Chop the broccoli** to ensure it's in small, digestible pieces for your dog.
2. **Cook Beef**: Heat the olive oil in a large skillet over medium heat. Add the ground beef and cook until it's browned and fully cooked, breaking it into small pieces as it cooks.
3. **Add Broccoli**: Once the beef is nearly cooked, add the chopped broccoli to the skillet. Cook together for 5 minutes, until the broccoli is tender.
4. **Scramble Eggs**: Beat the eggs in a bowl. Pour them over the beef and broccoli mixture in the skillet. Stir gently and cook until the eggs are fully scrambled and set.
5. **Cool Before Serving**: Allow the scramble to cool to room temperature to ensure it's safe for your dog.

PORK AND KALE SAUTÉ

Minced pork cooked with kale and a splash of coconut oil

Protein: 50% | Fat: 40% | Carbohydrates: 5% | Minerals and vitamins: 5%

🕐 25 min	🍲 48 oz	🍽 960 (20 per oz) kcal

INGREDIENTS

- 2 lbs minced pork
- 2 cups chopped kale, stems removed
- 2 tbsps coconut oil
- Water as needed (to help steam the kale)

DIRECTIONS

1. **Prep Ingredients:** Wash the kale thoroughly, remove the stems, and chop the leaves into bite-sized pieces.
2. **Heat Coconut Oil:** In a large skillet or sauté pan, heat the coconut oil over medium heat.
3. **Cook Pork:** Add the minced pork to the pan. Cook, stirring frequently to break up the meat, until the pork is fully cooked, about 10 minutes.
4. **Add Kale:** Mix in the chopped kale with the pork. Add 2 tbsps of water to help create steam (it will help the kale wilt and cook more evenly). Cook for 5 more minutes, until the kale is tender and bright green.
5. **Cool Before Serving:** Allow the sauté to cool to ensure it's safe for your dog.

GROUND BEEF AND SQUASH CASSEROLE

Ground beef baked with butternut squash and a sprinkle of sage

Protein: 50% | Fat: 40% | Carbohydrates: 5% | Minerals and vitamins: 5%

🕐 1 h	🍲 48 oz	🍽 1200 (25 per oz) kcal

INGREDIENTS

- 2 lbs ground beef
- 2 cups butternut squash, peeled and cubed
- 1 tsp dried sage
- 1 tbsp olive oil
- Water as needed

DIRECTIONS

1. **Preheat Oven:** Preheat your oven to 375°F (190°C).
2. **Prep Ingredients:** Peel and cube the butternut squash into small pieces.
3. **Cook Beef:** Heat olive oil in a skillet over medium heat. Add the beef and cook until browned, breaking it into small pieces as it cooks.
4. **Add Sage:** Sprinkle the dried sage over the cooked beef, mixing well to distribute the herb evenly.
5. **Layer Ingredients:** Layer the cooked ground beef and cubed butternut squash in a baking dish. Pour a little water into the dish (just enough to cover the bottom) to prevent sticking and help the squash cook evenly.
6. **Bake:** Cover the baking dish with foil and bake in the oven for 45 minutes, or until the squash is tender and the flavors have melded together.
7. **Cool Before Serving:** Cool the dish before serving it to your dog.

VENISON AND CRANBERRY MIX

Slow-cooked venison with cranberries and mashed parsnips

Protein: 60% | Fat: 25% | Carbohydrates: 10% | Minerals and vitamins: 5%

2 h	48 oz	960 (20 per oz) kcal

INGREDIENTS

- 2 lbs venison, cut into chunks
- 1 cup fresh or frozen cranberries
- 3 large parsnips, peeled and chopped
- 4 cups water or low-sodium beef broth
- 1 tbsp olive oil

DIRECTIONS

1. **Prep Ingredients:** Peel and chop the parsnips into cubes. If using fresh cranberries, rinse them thoroughly.
2. **Brown the Venison:** Heat the olive oil in a large pot over medium-high heat. Add the venison chunks and sear for 5-7 minutes.
3. **Add Cranberries and Broth:** Add the cranberries to the pot with the venison, then pour in the water or broth.
4. **Simmer:** Boil the mixture, then reduce the heat to low. Cover and let it simmer for 1.5 hours or until the venison is tender.
5. **Cook Parsnips:** In a separate pot, boil the chopped parsnips until soft, about 20-25 minutes.
6. **Mash Parsnips:** Drain the parsnips and mash them. To achieve a creamy texture, add a splash of the broth.
7. **Combine and Serve:** Add the mashed parsnips to the venison and cranberries, mixing well.
8. **Cool Before Serving:** Allow the dish to cool to room temperature to ensure it's safe for your dog.

LAMB BROTH BOWL

Bone-in lamb pieces simmered to make a broth, served with meat and vegetables

Protein: 40% | Fat: 35% | Carbohydrates: 20% | Minerals and vitamins: 5%

4 h	64 oz	1280 (20 per oz) kcal

INGREDIENTS

- 2 lbs of bone-in lamb pieces
- 1 large carrot, chopped
- 1 celery stalk, chopped
- 1 small sweet potato, peeled and cubed
- 6 cups water
- 1 tbsp apple cider vinegar (helps extract nutrients from bones)

DIRECTIONS

1. **Prep Ingredients:** Chop the carrot and celery into bite-sized pieces. Peel and cube the sweet potato.
2. **Simmer the Lamb:** Place the bone-in lamb pieces in a large pot. Add the chopped vegetables and 6 cups of water. Stir in the apple cider vinegar, which helps leach minerals from the bones.
3. **Cook Slowly:** Boil the mixture, then reduce the heat to a low simmer. Cover and let it cook for 3-4 hours.
4. **Remove Bones:** Carefully remove the lamb pieces from the broth after cooking. Remove all small bones and shred the meat.
5. **Strain Vegetables:** Remove and discard the cooked vegetables, leaving a clear broth.
6. **Combine Meat and Broth:** Return the shredded lamb meat to the broth.
7. **Cool Before Serving:** Allow the dish to cool to room temperature to ensure it's safe for your dog.

4.2. POULTRY DISHES

4.2.1. Poultry: A Peck of Perks for Your Pet

• *Lean and Mean Protein*: Poultry is a fantastic source of lean protein that helps your dog maintain strong muscles and a healthy weight. It's also gentle on their stomach, making it perfect for pups with a sensitive digestive system.

• *Vitamins and Minerals Galore*: Poultry isn't just about protein; it's also packed with essential vitamins like B3 (niacin), B6, and B12, which are crucial for brain health and converting food into energy. Plus, minerals like phosphorus and selenium keep your dog's bones strong and metabolism humming.

• *Easy on the Taste Buds*: Dogs love the mild taste of poultry, and it's often a hit even with the pickiest eaters. It's easy to cook and even easier to mix with various veggies and grains to create a meal that's as tasty as it is nutritious.

• *Heart Health Helper*: Poultry's lean nature helps manage cholesterol levels and supports heart health, making it an excellent choice for keeping your furry friend's ticker in top shape.

• *A Recipe for Every Dog*: Poultry is incredibly versatile and can be adapted to any dog's diet, including those on calorie-controlled diets or with specific health needs. Always consult with your vet to ensure you meet your dog's dietary requirements, especially if they have allergies or other health concerns.

Incorporating poultry into your homemade dog food recipes means providing your pet with a lean, delicious, and nutrient-rich ingredient. It's a simple way to show love through every meal you make, ensuring your pet is happy, healthy, and ready for any adventure!

4.2.2. Poultry Dishes Recipes

Check out the next pages for a bunch of tasty and well-balanced poultry recipes for your dog. It's your chance to become your furry friend's favorite chef!

CHICKEN AND RICE SIMMER

Boiled chicken breast shredded and mixed with cooked rice

Protein: 65% | Fat: 15% | Carbohydrates: 15% | Minerals and vitamins: 5%

 30 min   32 oz   640 (20 per oz) kcal

INGREDIENTS

- 16 oz chicken breast (boneless, skinless)
- 1 cup rice (white or brown, depending on your dog's ' dietary needs)
- 3 cups of water (for cooking rice)
- 1 tsp olive oil (optional, for added healthy fats)

DIRECTIONS

1. **Prep the Chicken:** Place the chicken breasts in a pot and cover with water. Bring to a boil, then reduce heat to a simmer. Cook for 20 minutes or until the chicken is thoroughly cooked.
2. **Cook the Rice:** Rinse the rice under cold water. In a separate pot, bring 3 cups of water to a boil. Add the rice and stir once. Reduce the heat to a low simmer and cover the pot. Cook about 15 minutes.
3. **Shred the Chicken:** Once cooked, remove the chicken from the pot, allow it to cool, and then shred it using two forks.
4. **Mix Ingredients:** Combine the shredded chicken and cooked rice in a large bowl. If desired, add a teaspoon of olive oil for extra healthy fats.
5. **Serve:** Let the mixture cool to room temperature before serving your dog.

TURKEY VEGGIE MASH

Ground turkey cooked with mashed sweet potatoes and green beans

Protein: 55% | Fat: 25% | Carbohydrates: 15% | Minerals and vitamins: 5%

 45 min   32 oz   680 (21.25 per oz) kcal

INGREDIENTS

- 16 oz ground turkey
- 2 medium sweet potatoes (about 12 oz total)
- 8 oz green beans, trimmed
- 2 tbsps olive oil
- 1 cup water

DIRECTIONS

1. **Prep the Veggies:** Peel the sweet potatoes and cut them into chunks. Trim the ends off the green beans and cut them into bite-sized pieces.
2. **Cook the Sweet Potatoes:** Place sweet potato in a pot, cover with water, and boil. Reduce heat to a simmer and cook until tender, for 15-20 min.
3. **Cook the Turkey:** Heat a large skillet over medium heat. Add the turkey and cook until browned. Break it up with a spoon as it cooks, for 10 min
4. **Steam the Green Beans:** In another pot, steam the green beans until tender but still crisp, for 7-10 min.
5. **Mash the Sweet Potatoes:** Drain and return them to the pot. Add 1 tbsp of olive oil and mash until smooth.
6. **Combine Ingredients:** In a large bowl, mix the ground turkey, mashed sweet potatoes, and steamed green beans. Stir in the remaining tablespoon of olive oil to add healthy fats and improve the meal's palatability.
7. **Serve:** Allow the mash to cool to room temperature before serving to your dog.

DUCK AND PEA PATTIES

Ground duck mixed with peas and formed into small patties

Protein: 50% | Fat: 35% | Carbohydrates: 10% | Minerals and vitamins: 5%

 35 min 30 oz  750 (25 per oz) kcal

INGREDIENTS

- 20 oz ground duck
- 10 oz peas (fresh or frozen)
- 2 tbsps ground flaxseed (optional, for binding and added fiber)
- 1 tbsp olive oil (for cooking)

DIRECTIONS

1. **Prep the Ingredients:** If using frozen peas, thaw them beforehand. If using fresh peas, ensure they are shelled and ready to mix.
2. **Mix the Ingredients:** In a large bowl, combine the ground duck, peas, and flaxseed. Mix thoroughly to ensure the peas are evenly distributed throughout the duck mixture.
3. **Form Patties:** Divide the mixture into small, even portions — about the size of a golf ball — and flatten them into patties.
4. **Cook the Patties:** Heat olive oil in a skillet over medium heat. Place the patties in the skillet, cooking each side for about 4-5 minutes or until fully cooked and slightly golden outside.
5. **Cool Before Serving:** Allow the patties to cool on a paper towel to absorb excess oil before serving your dog.

SIMPLE CHICKEN LIVER FRY

Chicken liver quickly sautéed and cooled before serving

Protein: 65% | Fat: 30% | Carbohydrates: 1% | Minerals and vitamins: 4%

10 min 16 oz 720 (45 per oz) kcal

INGREDIENTS

- 16 oz chicken liver
- 1 tbsp olive oil

DIRECTIONS

1. **Clean the Liver:** Rinse the chicken livers under cold water, pat them dry with paper towels, and trim any fat or connective tissue.
2. **Heat the Pan:** Heat olive oil in a large skillet over medium heat until hot but not smoking.
3. **Cook the Liver:** Add the chicken livers to the skillet in a single layer. Cook for 3-4 minutes on each side until they are no longer pink in the middle. Ensure they are cooked through but not overcooked, as they can become tough.
4. **Cool Before Serving:** Remove the chicken livers from the skillet and let them cool on a plate. Once cooled, chop them into bite-sized pieces appropriate for your dog's size.

QUAIL AND APPLE MIX

Chopped quail meat cooked with diced apples

Protein: 60% | Fat: 25% | Carbohydrates: 10% | Minerals and vitamins: 5%

| 🕐 25 min | 🍽 24 oz | 🍲 600 (25 per oz) kcal |

INGREDIENTS

- 16 oz quail meat, boneless and skinless, chopped
- 8 oz apples, peeled and diced
- 1 tbsp coconut oil

DIRECTIONS

1. **Prep the Ingredients:** Peel and dice the apples into small, bite-sized pieces. Chop the quail meat into similarly sized pieces to ensure even cooking.
2. **Heat the Pan:** In a skillet, heat the coconut oil over medium heat until melted and hot.
3. **Cook the Quail:** Add the quail to the skillet. Cook for about 10 min, stirring occasionally, until the meat is browned and cooked through.
4. **Add the Apples:** Add the diced apples to the skillet with the quail. Cook together for 5 minutes until the apples are soft but not mushy.
5. **Cool Before Serving:** Remove the skillet from heat and allow the mixture to cool to room temperature. Ensure the pieces are appropriately sized for your dog to eat safely.

TURKEY AND CARROT BALLS

Ground turkey and grated carrots mixed and formed into small balls

Protein: 58% | Fat: 30% | Carbohydrates: 10% | Minerals and vitamins: 2%

| 🕐 30 min | 🍽 30 oz | 🍲 900 (30 per oz) kcal |

INGREDIENTS

- 20 oz ground turkey
- 10 oz carrots, peeled and finely grated
- 2 eggs (to help bind the mixture)
- 1 tbsp parsley, chopped (optional, for added flavor and vitamins)
- 1 tbsp olive oil (for cooking)

DIRECTIONS

1. **Prep the Ingredients:** Peel and grate the carrots finely. Chop the parsley if using.
2. **Mix Ingredients:** In a large bowl, combine the ground turkey, grated carrots, eggs, and parsley. Mix well.
3. **Form the Balls:** Scoop out the mixture and form it into small balls. The size of the balls should be appropriate for your dog's size.
4. **Cook the Balls:** Heat olive oil in a large skillet over medium heat. Add the turkey and carrot balls, cooking in batches if necessary to avoid overcrowding. Cook each ball for 4-5 minutes on each side or until golden brown and cooked through.
5. **Cool Before Serving:** Allow the balls to cool to room temperature before serving to ensure they are safe for your dog to eat.

CHICKEN BREAST STRIPS

Boiled chicken breast cut into strips and served with a sprinkle of parsley

Protein: 80% | Fat: 15% | Carbohydrates: 3% | Minerals and vitamins: 2%

20 min	24 oz	720 (30 per oz) kcal

INGREDIENTS

• 24 oz chicken breast (boneless and skinless)
• 1/4 cup fresh parsley, finely chopped
• Water for boiling

DIRECTIONS

1. **Prepare Chicken:** Rinse the chicken breasts under cold water and pat them dry with paper towels.
2. **Boil the Chicken:** Place the chicken breasts in a large pot and cover them with water. Boil it, then reduce the heat to a low simmer. Cover the pot and cook the chicken for 15 minutes.
3. **Cool and Slice:** Remove the chicken from the water and let it cool to the touch. Once cooled, slice the chicken into thin strips suitable for your dog's size.
4. **Add Parsley:** Sprinkle the finely chopped parsley over the chicken strips for added flavor and nutrients.
5. **Serve:** Cool the chicken to room temperature before serving to your dog.

DUCK AND PUMPKIN PUREE

Shredded duck cooked with pumpkin puree for a soft meal

Protein: 60% | Fat: 30% | Carbohydrates: 8% | Minerals and vitamins: 2%

45 min	28 oz	980 (35 per oz) kcal

INGREDIENTS

• 20 oz duck breast, skin removed
• 8 oz canned pumpkin puree (ensure it's 100% pumpkin with no additives)
• 1 tbsp olive oil
• Water for cooking

DIRECTIONS

1. **Prepare the Duck:** Cut the duck breast into small pieces, removing fat and skin.
2. **Cook the Duck:** Heat the olive oil in a medium skillet over medium heat. Add the duck and cook for 10-12 minutes. Ensure the duck is cooked through with no pink remaining.
3. **Puree the Cooked Duck:** Allow the duck to cool slightly, then transfer it to a food processor or blender. Blend until the duck is shredded or reaches a desired consistency.
4. **Mix with Pumpkin:** Combine the shredded duck with the pumpkin puree in a large mixing bowl. Stir until well incorporated.
5. **Final Prep:** If the mixture is too thick, add a small amount of water to reach a softer consistency. Ensure the mixture is cool before serving.

TURKEY AND RICE SOUP

Ground turkey cooked with rice in a simple broth

Protein: 50% | Fat: 20% | Carbohydrates: 25% | Minerals and vitamins: 5%

⏱ 45 min	🍲 50 oz	🍽 800 (20 per oz) kcal

INGREDIENTS

- 16 oz ground turkey
- 1 cup uncooked rice
- 6 cups of water or unsalted chicken broth
- 1 carrot, diced (optional for added nutrients and flavor)
- 1 tsp of olive oil (to cook the turkey)

DIRECTIONS

1. **Cook the Turkey:** Heat the olive oil in a large pot over medium heat. Add the ground turkey and cook until it's browned and fully cooked, breaking it up as it cooks.
2. **Add Water/Broth and Rice:** Once the turkey is cooked, add the water or unsalted chicken broth to the pot and the uncooked rice. Stir to combine.
3. **Simmer:** Bring the mixture to a boil, then reduce the heat to a simmer. If using, add the diced carrot now. Cover and let it simmer for about 30 minutes or until the rice is tender and the soup has thickened slightly.
4. **Cool and Serve:** Allow the soup to cool down to room temperature before serving to ensure it's safe for your dog to eat.

CHICKEN AND ZUCCHINI SAUTÉ

Chicken breast cooked with zucchini in a light olive oil

Protein: 70% | Fat: 25% | Carbohydrates: 4% | Minerals and vitamins: 1%

⏱ 25 min	🍲 32 oz	🍽 640 (20 per oz) kcal

INGREDIENTS

- 20 oz chicken breast, cut into bite-sized pieces
- 12 oz zucchini, sliced into half-moons
- 2 tbsp olive oil
- Water (optional, if additional moisture is needed)

DIRECTIONS

1. **Prep Ingredients:** Rinse the chicken and pat dry. Cut into small pieces suitable for your dog. Wash the zucchini and slice into thin half-moons.
2. **Heat Olive Oil:** In a large skillet, heat the olive oil over medium heat.
3. **Cook Chicken:** Add the chicken pieces to the skillet and sauté until they are golden and nearly cooked through for 10 minutes.
4. **Add Zucchini:** Add the zucchini to the skillet with the chicken. Sauté together for 10-15 minutes until the zucchini is soft and the chicken is fully cooked.
5. **Simmer:** If the mixture seems dry, add a small amount of water to moisten the pan.
6. **Cool Before Serving:** Allow the sauté to cool to room temperature to ensure it's safe for your dog to eat.

TURKEY GIBLET MIX

Turkey giblets boiled and chopped finely, served with cooked barley

Protein: 65% | Fat: 25% | Carbohydrates: 8% | Minerals and vitamins: 2%

 50 min

 36 oz

900 (25 per oz) kcal

INGREDIENTS

• 20 oz turkey giblets (heart, liver, and gizzard), cleaned and rinsed
• 16 oz barley, rinsed
• 6 cups of water (for cooking barley)
• 2 cups of water (for boiling giblets)

DIRECTIONS

1. **Prep Giblets:** Place the turkey giblets in a pot and cover with 2 cups of water. Bring to a boil, then reduce the heat and simmer for 30 minutes until they are tender.
2. **Cook Barley:** Simultaneously, in another pot, add the rinsed barley and 6 cups of water. Bring to a boil, then reduce the heat and simmer for 30 minutes until the barley is cooked and tender.
3. **Chop Giblets:** Once the giblets are cooked, drain, and let them cool slightly. Then, finely chop them to ensure they are in small, manageable pieces for your dog.
4. **Combine Ingredients:** Mix the chopped giblets and cooked barley together in a large bowl.
5. **Cool and Serve:** Cool the mixture to room temperature before serving.

DUCK AND SWEET POTATO BAKE

Chopped duck and sweet potatoes baked until soft

Protein: 55% | Fat: 35% | Carbohydrates: 8% | Minerals and vitamins: 2%

 1 h

 32 oz

960 (30 per oz) kcal

INGREDIENTS

• 20 oz duck meat, chopped into small pieces
• 12 oz sweet potatoes, peeled and cubed
• 2 tbsps olive oil
• 1/2 cup water

DIRECTIONS

1. **Preheat Oven:** Preheat your oven to 375°F (190°C).
2. **Prep Ingredients:** Peel and cube the sweet potatoes into small pieces. Chop the duck, ensuring the pieces are small enough for your dog.
3. **Mix Ingredients:** Combine the duck, sweet potatoes, and olive oil in a baking dish. Toss everything together so that the oil lightly coats the ingredients.
4. **Add Water:** Pour the water into the baking dish to keep it moist while baking and prevent it from drying.
5. **Bake:** Cover the dish with foil and bake in the oven for about 45 minutes. Then, remove the foil and bake for an additional 15 minutes.
6. **Cool and Serve:** Allow the dish to cool to room temperature before serving to ensure it's safe for your dog to eat.

CHICKEN HEART STEW

Chicken hearts simmered with carrots and celery

Protein: 70% | Fat: 20% | Carbohydrates: 6% | Minerals and vitamins: 4%

 40 min | 32 oz | 800 (25 per oz) kcal

INGREDIENTS

- 16 oz chicken hearts, cleaned and halved
- 8 oz carrots, peeled and sliced
- 8 oz celery, sliced
- 4 cups water or unsalted chicken broth
- 1 tbsp olive oil

DIRECTIONS

1. **Prep Ingredients:** Rinse the chicken hearts under cold water, trim off any fat, and cut them in half. Peel and slice the carrots and celery into bite-sized pieces.
2. **Heat the Olive Oil:** Heat the olive oil over medium heat in a large pot.
3. **Sauté Vegetables:** Add the carrots and celery to the pot and sauté for 5 minutes until they soften.
4. **Add Chicken Hearts:** Add the chicken hearts to the pot and cook for another 5 minutes, stirring frequently.
5. **Add Water or Broth:** Pour in the water or unsalted chicken broth, covering the ingredients. Bring to a boil, then reduce the heat and simmer for about 30 minutes.
6. **Cool and Serve:** Let the stew cool down to room temperature before serving to ensure it is safe for your dog to consume.

TURKEY AND SPINACH QUICK FRY

Ground turkey sautéed with spinach for a quick meal

Protein: 60% | Fat: 30% | Carbohydrates: 5% | Minerals and vitamins: 5%

 15 min | 40 oz | 800 (20 per oz) kcal

INGREDIENTS

- 2 pounds ground turkey
- 2 cups fresh spinach, chopped
- 1 tbsp olive oil

DIRECTIONS

1. **Heat Oil:** Heat the olive oil over medium heat in a large skillet.
2. **Cook Turkey:** Add the ground turkey to the skillet. Break it up with a spatula and cook until it is browned and no longer pink, about 8-10 minutes.
3. **Add Spinach:** Once the turkey is nearly cooked, add the chopped spinach to the skillet. Stir well until the spinach is wilted and integrated into the turkey, about 2-3 minutes.
4. **Cool and Serve:** Allow the mixture to cool to room temperature before serving to ensure it's safe for your dog.

CHICKEN AND APPLE QUICK COOK

Diced Chicken with Apple Slices

Protein: 70% | Fat: 20% | Carbohydrates: 9% | Minerals and vitamins: 1%

20 min	32 oz	 750 (25 per oz) kcal

INGREDIENTS

- 20 oz chicken breast, diced
- 10 oz apples, cored and thinly sliced (choose a sweet variety like Fuji or Gala)
- 1 tbsp olive oil
- Water (optional, if needed for cooking)

DIRECTIONS

1. **Prep Chicken:** Dice the chicken breast into small, bite-sized pieces suitable for your dog.
2. **Prep Apples:** Core the apples and slice them into thin pieces. Choosing dog-friendly varieties like Gala or Fuji can add a natural sweetness.
3. **Cook Chicken:** Heat a skillet over medium heat. If using, add olive oil to the skillet to help prevent sticking, and add a bit of healthy fat to the diet. Add the diced chicken to the skillet. Cook for about 8-10 minutes, stirring occasionally, until the chicken is thoroughly cooked and no longer pink inside.
4. **Add Apples:** Once the chicken is nearly done, add the sliced apples to the skillet. Cook together for an additional 5 minutes until the apples are soft and the chicken is fully cooked.
5. **Cool and Serve:** Remove the skillet from heat and allow the mixture to cool down to room temperature before serving to ensure it is safe for your dog to eat.
6. **Serve:** You can serve this meal as is, or you can mix it with your dog's regular kibble to enhance their meal's flavor and nutritional value.

TURKEY AND BEET BLEND

Ground turkey cooked with diced beets

Protein: 60% | Fat: 25% | Carbohydrates: 10% | Minerals and vitamins: 5%

35 min	32 oz	960 (30 per oz) kcal

INGREDIENTS

- 20 oz ground turkey
- 12 oz fresh beets, peeled and diced
- 1 tbsp coconut oil

DIRECTIONS

1. **Prep the Beets:** Peel the beets and dice them into small, bite-sized pieces to ensure they cook thoroughly and are easy for your dog to eat.
2. **Cook the Turkey:** In a large skillet, heat the coconut oil over medium heat. Add the ground turkey and cook, stirring frequently, until it's browned and no longer pink, about 7-10 minutes.
3. **Add Beets:** Once the turkey is cooked, add the diced beets to the skillet. Stir to combine with the turkey.
4. **Simmer:** Cover the skillet, reduce the heat to low, and let simmer for about 20 minutes, or until the beets are tender and fully cooked.
5. **Cool Before Serving:** Allow the mixture to cool to room temperature before serving to ensure it's safe for your dog to eat.

CHICKEN AND CUCUMBER SALAD

Cooked chicken breast cooled and mixed with cucumber slices

Protein: 75% | Fat: 20% | Carbohydrates: 4% | Minerals and vitamins: 1%

 20 min   24 oz   480 (20 per oz) kcal

INGREDIENTS

- 16 oz chicken breast
- 8 oz cucumber, peeled and thinly sliced
- 1 tbsp olive oil (optional, to add healthy fats)
- Water for boiling chicken

DIRECTIONS

1. **Cook the Chicken:** Place the chicken in a pot and cover with water. Bring to a boil and then reduce to a simmer. Cook until the chicken is thoroughly done, for 12-15 minutes.
2. **Cool the Chicken:** Remove the chicken from the water and let it cool completely. Then, shred or chop the chicken into bite-sized pieces.
3. **Prepare the Cucumber:** Peel the cucumber and slice it thinly. If your dog prefers smaller pieces, you can dice the cucumber instead of slicing.
4. **Mix Ingredients:** Combine the cooled chicken and cucumber slices in a large bowl. Drizzle with olive oil, if using, to add healthy fats and improve the overall palatability.
5. **Serve:** Ensure the salad is at room temperature before serving.

DUCK AND CARROT STICKS

Shredded duck cooked with carrot sticks

Protein: 65% | Fat: 30% | Carbohydrates: 3% | Minerals and vitamins: 2%

35 min   30 oz   750 (25 per oz) kcal

INGREDIENTS

- 20 oz duck breast, skin removed and shredded
- 10 oz carrots, peeled and cut into sticks
- 1 tbsp coconut oil

DIRECTIONS

1. **Prep the Duck:** Rinse the. Remove excess fat and the skin.
2. **Cook the Duck:** Heat the coconut oil over medium heat in a skillet. Add the duck and cook until browned, 8-10 minutes on each side. Remove from heat and let cool slightly. Then, shred the meat using two forks.
3. **Prep the Carrots:** Peel and cut them into stick shapes.
4. **Combine Ingredients:** In the skillet, add the carrot and a splash of water to steam them. Cook for 5 minutes.
5. **Mix Duck and Carrots:** Add the duck back into the skillet with the carrot and stir to combine over low heat for 2-3 minutes.
6. **Cool Before Serving:** Allow the mixture to cool to room temperature before serving to ensure it's safe for your dog to eat.

CHICKEN GIZZARD GOULASH

Chicken gizzards cooked with a mix of vegetables

Protein: 60% | Fat: 25% | Carbohydrates: 10% | Minerals and vitamins: 5%

 45 min   33 oz    640 (20 per oz) kcal

INGREDIENTS

- 16 oz chicken gizzards, cleaned and chopped
- 4 oz carrots, peeled and diced
- 4 oz green beans, trimmed and chopped
- 4 oz potatoes, peeled and cubed
- 4 oz peas
- 1 tbsp olive oil
- 4 cups of water or unsalted chicken broth

DIRECTIONS

1. **Prep Ingredients:** Clean the chicken gizzards by trimming excess fat and chopping them into bite-sized pieces. Peel and dice the carrots, peel, and cube the potatoes, trim and chop the green beans.
2. **Cook Gizzards:** Heat olive oil in a large pot over medium heat. Add the chicken gizzards and cook until they start to brown for 10 min.
3. **Add Vegetables:** Add carrots, green beans, and potatoes to the pot. Stir to mix with the gizzards.
4. **Add Water or Broth:** Pour in the water or unsalted chicken broth, ensuring the ingredients are fully submerged.
5. **Simmer:** Boi it, then reduce heat and simmer for 30 minutes, until the vegetables are tender, and the gizzards are cooked.
6. **Add Peas:** Stir in the peas and cook for 5 minutes.
7. **Cool Before Serving:** Cool it to room temperature before serving.

TURKEY AND PUMPKIN CUBES

Turkey breast cooked and cubed with baked pumpkin

Protein: 70% | Fat: 15% | Carbohydrates: 13% | Minerals and vitamins: 2%

 1 h   36 oz   720 (20 per oz) kcal

INGREDIENTS

- 24 oz turkey breast, boneless and skinless
- 12 oz pumpkin, peeled and cubed
- 1 tbsp olive oil (for cooking turkey)
- Water (for boiling turkey)

DIRECTIONS

1. **Prep the Pumpkin:** Preheat your oven to 375°F (190°C). Peel the pumpkin and cut it into small, bite-sized cubes.
2. **Bake the Pumpkin:** Spread the pumpkin cubes on a baking sheet and roast in the oven for 30-40 minutes.
3. **Cook the Turkey:** Place the turkey breast in a pot and cover it with water. Bring to a boil, then reduce the heat and simmer until the turkey is fully cooked about 20-25 minutes.
4. **Cube the Turkey:** Once cooked, remove the turkey from the pot and let it cool. Then, dice the turkey into bite-sized cubes.
5. **Combine and Mix:** Mix the cooked turkey cubes with the roasted pumpkin cubes in a large bowl. Drizzle with a tablespoon of olive oil to enhance flavor and add healthy fats.
6. **Cool Before Serving:** Allow the mixture to cool to room temperature before serving to ensure it's safe for your dog to eat.

4.3. FISH DISHES

4.3.1. Why Fish Dishes Are Fantastic for Your Furry Friend's Diet

• *Superb Source of Omega-3 Fatty Acids*: Fish is loaded with omega-3 fatty acids, heroes for your dog's skin and coat. These nutrients help make your dog's coat glossy and reduce annoying skin itchiness. Plus, omega-3s ease joint pain, which is excellent news for senior dogs.

• *Gentle on the Tummy*: Fish is a fantastic choice if your pooch has a sensitive stomach. It's packed with high-quality protein that dogs can easily digest, making mealtime a breeze for their bellies.

• *Yummy and Exciting*: Let's face it, dogs love tasty food, and fish is often a big hit. It's a wonderful way to spice up their diet with new flavors, which is perfect for picky eaters or those with a dwindling appetite.

• *Keeps the Pounds Off*: Fish is typically low in fat and calories, making it an excellent option for managing your dog's weight. This is particularly important for dogs that aren't active or those on a diet.

• *Packed with Important Nutrients*: Fish isn't just tasty; it's also rich in vitamins and minerals like vitamin D for strong bones and B vitamins for a healthy metabolism and nerves.

• *Brain Booster*: Fish's DHA helps with brain and vision development in puppies. It also supports brain health in older dogs, keeping them sharp and attentive.

Tips for Serving Fish

Cooking fish properly is key to keeping your dog safe as well. Always remove all bones to avoid any dangers and choose fish species known to be low in mercury and other contaminants.

Fish dishes can be a regular part of your pet's meal or just a treat - either way, your furry friend is sure to wag his tail with joy!

4.3.2. Fish Dishes Recipes

Below, you will find many delicious and healthy fish recipes for your dog!

HADDOCK AND CARROT BAKE

Baked haddock fillets with sliced carrots

Protein: 65% | Fat: 15% | Carbohydrates: 15% | Minerals and vitamins: 5%

⏱ 40 min	🍲 30 oz	🍽 600 (20 per oz) kcal

INGREDIENTS

- 20 oz haddock fillets
- 10 oz carrots, peeled and thinly sliced
- 1 tbsp olive oil (to grease the baking dish)

DIRECTIONS

1. **Preheat Oven:** Preheat your oven to 375°F (190°C).
2. **Prepare Ingredients:** Rinse the haddock fillets under cold water and pat dry with paper towels. Peel the carrots and slice them thinly.
3. **Grease Baking Dish:** Lightly grease a baking dish with olive oil to prevent sticking.
4. **Arrange Fillets and Carrots:** Place the haddock fillets in the baking dish and scatter the sliced carrots around and over the fillets.
5. **Bake:** Cover the dish with aluminum foil and bake in the preheated oven for 25-30 minutes, or until the haddock is cooked through and flakes easily with a fork, and the carrots are tender.
6. **Cool Before Serving:** Allow the dish to cool to room temperature before serving to ensure it's safe for your dog to eat.

WHITEFISH AND PUMPKIN PUREE

Steamed whitefish flaked and mixed with pumpkin puree

Protein: 65% | Fat: 20% | Carbohydrates: 10% | Minerals and vitamins: 5%

⏱ 40 min	🍲 28 oz	🍽 560 (20 per oz) kcal

INGREDIENTS

- 16 oz whitefish (such as cod, haddock, or pollock), deboned
- 12 oz canned pure pumpkin puree (ensure it's 100% pumpkin with no additives or sugar)
- Water for steaming

DIRECTIONS

1. **Prep the Fish:** Rinse the whitefish under cold water and check for any remaining bones.
2. **Steam the Fish:** Place the fish in a steamer over boiling water and cover. Steam for about 10-15 minutes, or until the fish is fully cooked and flakes easily with a fork.
3. **Flake the Fish:** Once cooked, remove the fish from the steamer and let it cool slightly. Use a fork to flake the fish into small pieces.
4. **Mix with Pumpkin:** In a mixing bowl, combine the flaked fish with the canned pumpkin puree. Stir until well mixed.
5. **Cool Before Serving:** Allow the mixture to cool to room temperature before serving to ensure it's safe for your dog to eat.

TROUT AND APPLE MIX

Cooked trout flaked and mixed with finely diced apples

Protein: 60% | Fat: 30% | Carbohydrates: 8% | Minerals and vitamins: 2%

| 🕐 30 min | 🍽 24 oz | 🍲 600 (25 per oz) kcal |

INGREDIENTS

- 16 oz trout fillets, deboned
- 8 oz apples, cored and finely diced (choose a sweet variety like Fuji or Gala for better flavor)
- 1 tbsp olive oil (for cooking trout)

DIRECTIONS

1. **Prep the Trout:** Rinse the trout fillets under cold water and pat dry. Check for any bones and remove them.
2. **Cook the Trout:** Heat the olive oil in a skillet over medium heat. Add the trout fillets and cook for 5-7 minutes on each side or until the fish flakes easily with a fork. Remove from heat and let cool.
3. **Prep the Apples:** While the trout is cooking, core and finely dice the apples. To prevent browning, sprinkle a little lemon juice on the diced apples.
4. **Flake the Trout:** Once cooled, use a fork to flake the trout into small, bite-sized pieces.
5. **Mix Ingredients:** In a large mixing bowl, combine the flaked trout and diced apples. Mix to combine without breaking the apple pieces.
6. **Cool Before Serving:** Allow the mixture to cool to room temperature before serving to ensure it's safe for your dog to eat.

COD AND BROCCOLI BOWL

Steamed cod served with finely chopped steamed broccoli

Protein: 70% | Fat: 15% | Carbohydrates: 12% | Minerals and vitamins: 3%

| 🕐 25 min | 🍽 30 oz | 🍲 450 (15 per oz) kcal |

INGREDIENTS

- 20 oz cod fillets
- 10 oz fresh broccoli, chopped into small florets
- Water for steaming

DIRECTIONS

1. **Prep Ingredients:** Rinse the cod fillets and broccoli under cold water. Chop the broccoli into small, bite-sized florets.
2. **Steam Cod:** Place the cod fillets in a steaming basket over boiling water. Cover and steam for 10-12 minutes.
3. **Steam Broccoli:** If there's room, steam the chopped broccoli in a separate steamer or the same one for 5-7 minutes until tender but still firm to preserve the nutrients.
4. **Flake Cod:** Once the cod is cooked, remove it from the steamer and let it cool slightly. Use a fork to flake the cod into small pieces.
5. **Combine Ingredients:** Mix the flaked cod with the broccoli in a bowl.
6. **Cool Before Serving:** Allow the bowl to cool to room temperature before serving to ensure it's safe for your dog to eat.

CATFISH AND CUCUMBER COOL DOWN

Cooked catfish served with fresh cucumber slices

Protein: 70% | Fat: 25% | Carbohydrates: 4% | Minerals and vitamins: 1%

25 min	28 oz	560 (20 per oz) kcal

INGREDIENTS

- 18 oz catfish fillets
- 10 oz cucumbers, peeled and thinly sliced
- 1 tbsp olive oil (for cooking)

DIRECTIONS

1. **Prep the Catfish:** Rinse the fillets under cold water and pat them dry. Check for any bones and remove them if found.
2. **Cook the Catfish:** Heat olive oil in a non-stick skillet over medium heat. Place the catfish fillets in the skillet and cook for 5-7 minutes on each side, until the fish is opaque and flakes easily with a fork.
3. **Prep the Cucumber:** Peel the cucumbers and slice them thinly.
4. **Cool the Catfish:** Once cooked, remove the catfish from the skillet and let it cool to room temperature. Then, flake the fish into bite-sized pieces, ensuring no bones.
5. **Combine Ingredients:** Mix the flaked catfish with the sliced cucumbers in a large mixing bowl.
6. Serve: Ensure the mixture is at room temperature or slightly cool before serving to your dog to ensure it's safe to eat.

ANCHOVY AND SWEET PEA MASH

Anchovies mashed with sweet peas and a touch of olive oil

Protein: 55% | Fat: 35% | Carbohydrates: 8% | Minerals and vitamins:25%

15 min	 20 oz	400 (20 per oz) kcal

INGREDIENTS

- 10 oz canned anchovies in water, drained
- 10 oz fresh or frozen sweet peas
- 1 tbsp olive oil

DIRECTIONS

1. **Prep the Peas:** If using frozen peas, bring a small pot of water to a boil and add the peas. Cook for 3-5 minutes until they are tender. If using fresh peas, increase cooking time slightly until peas are soft.
2. **Mash the Anchovies:** While the peas are cooking, place the drained anchovies in a mixing bowl and use a fork to mash them into a paste.
3. **Drain and Mash Peas:** Once the peas are cooked, drain them, and add to the bowl with the mashed anchovies.
4. **Combine Ingredients with Olive Oil:** Add a tablespoon of olive oil to the anchovies and peas. Use the fork or a potato masher to mash the ingredients together until you achieve a consistent mash.
5. **Cool Before Serving:** Let the mash cool to room temperature before serving to ensure it's safe for your dog.

SNAPPER AND SPINACH

Steamed snapper fillets served with wilted spinach.

Protein: 70% | Fats: 20% | Carbohydrates: 5% | Minerals and vitamins: 5%

🕐 25 min	🌡️ 30 oz	🍽️ 600 (20 per oz) kcal

INGREDIENTS

- 20 oz snapper fillets
- 10 oz fresh spinach
- 1 tbsp olive oil (for cooking spinach)

DIRECTIONS

1. **Prep Snapper:** Rinse the snapper fillets under cold water and pat them dry with paper towels. Ensure there are no bones.
2. **Steam Snapper:** Place the snapper fillets in a steamer over boiling water. Cover and steam for 10-12 minutes.
3. **Prep Spinach:** Wash the spinach thoroughly while the snapper is steaming. Heat olive oil in a large skillet over medium heat. Add the spinach and cook until it just begins to wilt about 3-5 minutes. Avoid overcooking to maintain nutrients.
4. **Serve:** Arrange the steamed snapper on a plate and surround it with the wilted spinach. Ensure the food is cool enough to be safely consumed by your dog before serving.

POLLOCK AND PARSLEY POT

Poached pollock flaked and tossed with fresh parsley..

Protein: 70% | Fats: 15% | Carbohydrates: 10% | Minerals and vitamins: 5%

🕐 20 min	🌡️ 32 oz	🍽️ 640 (20 per oz) kcal

INGREDIENTS

- 24 oz pollock fillets
- 8 oz fresh parsley, finely chopped
- Water for poaching

DIRECTIONS

1. **Prep Pollock:** Rinse the fillets under cold water and pat them dry with paper towels. Check for bones and remove any that are found.
2. **Poach Pollock:** Fill a large skillet or pot with enough water to cover the fillets. Bring the water to a simmer, then add the pollock. Poach the fillets for 10-12 minutes or until the fish is opaque and flakes easily with a fork.
3. **Prep Parsley:** Rinse and finely chop the fresh parsley.
4. **Flake and Mix:** Remove the pollock from the water and let it cool slightly. Once cool enough to handle, use a fork to flake the fish into small pieces. In a large bowl, combine the flaked pollock with the chopped parsley. Mix gently to combine.
5. **Serve:** Check the temperature of the pollock and parsley mixture to ensure it's safe for your dog to eat and serve.

SOLE AND ZUCCHINI SLICES

Grilled sole fillets served with thin slices of cooked zucchini

Protein: 70% | Fats: 15% | Carbohydrates: 10% | Minerals and vitamins: 5%

 25 min | 30 oz | 450 (15 per oz) kcal

INGREDIENTS

- 20 oz sole fillets
- 10 oz zucchini
- 1 tbsp olive oil (for grilling and cooking)

DIRECTIONS

1. **Prep Sole Fillets:** Rinse the sole fillets under cold water and pat them dry with paper towels. Check for any bones.
2. **Grill Sole Fillets:** Brush a grill pan or skillet with olive oil and heat over medium-high heat. Place the sole fillets in the pan and grill for 3-4 minutes on each side.
3. **Prep Zucchini:** Rinse the zucchini and slice it thinly.
4. **Cook Zucchini:** In another skillet, heat a small amount of olive oil over medium heat. Add the zucchini slices and sauté for 5-7 minutes, turning occasionally, until they are tender and lightly browned.
5. **Serve:** Arrange the grilled sole fillets on a plate and surround them with the sautéed zucchini slices. Allow the dish to cool to a safe temperature before serving to your dog.

HALIBUT AND RICE PILAF

Steamed halibut flaked into a simple pilaf made with rice and a bit of turmeric

Protein: 50% | Fats: 15% | Carbohydrates: 30% | Minerals and vitamins: 5%

 35 min | 32 oz | 640 (20 per oz) kcal

INGREDIENTS

- 16 oz halibut fillets
- 12 oz white rice
- 4 cups water (for cooking rice)
- 1 tsp turmeric
- 1 tbsp olive oil (for rice)

DIRECTIONS

1. **Cook Rice:** Rinse the rice under cold water. In a medium pot, combine the rice, 4 cups of water, turmeric, and olive oil. Bring to a boil, then reduce the heat to low, cover, and simmer for 18-20 minutes until the rice is tender and all the water has been absorbed.
2. **Prep Halibut:** Rinse the fillets under cold water and pat dry. Steam the halibut in a steamer over boiling water for 10-12 minutes.
3. **Flake Halibut:** Remove the halibut from the steamer and let it cool slightly. Flake the fish into small pieces, ensuring there are no bones.
4. **Combine Ingredients:** Cool the rice, fluff it with a fork and mix in the flaked halibut. Stir to combine.
5. **Serve:** Cool the pilaf to room temperature before serving.

SALMON SKIN CRISPS

Baked salmon skin until crispy, served as a treat

Protein: 58% | Fats: 40% | Carbohydrates: 1% | Minerals and vitamins: 1%

25 min	16 oz	480 (30 per oz) kcal

INGREDIENTS

- 16 oz fresh salmon skin (skin from approximately 2 large salmon fillets)

DIRECTIONS

1. **Prep Oven and Baking Sheet:** Preheat oven to 375°F (190°C) and line a baking sheet with parchment paper.
2. **Prep Salmon Skin:** Rinse and pat dry the salmon skin to remove scales and moisture. Cut into strips or squares as desired.
3. **Season (Optional):** Sprinkle with parsley or turmeric for added flavor; avoid salt or harmful spices.
4. **Bake:** Arrange skin pieces skin-side down on the baking sheet. Bake for 20-25 minutes until crispy and golden.
5. **Cool and Serve:** Let the crisps cool on a wire rack to maintain their crispiness. Once cooled, serve.
6. **Storage:** Leftovers can be stored in an airtight container in the fridge for up to 5 days or frozen for up to a month.

PERCH AND PEA PODS

Lightly cooked perch mixed with whole pea pods for a crunchy and protein-rich dish

Protein: 65% | Fats: 20% | Carbohydrates: 10% | Minerals and vitamins: 5%

15 min	32 oz	480 (15 per oz) kcal

INGREDIENTS

- 24 oz perch fillets, deboned and cut into bite-sized pieces
- 8 oz fresh pea pods, ends trimmed
- 1 tbsp olive oil (optional, for cooking)

DIRECTIONS

1. **Prep Perch:** Ensure the perch is fresh and deboned. Cut into bite-sized pieces suitable for your dog.
2. **Prep Pea Pods:** Trim and wash the pea pods thoroughly.
3. **Cook Perch:** In a non-stick skillet over medium heat, cook the perch pieces with olive oil for 5-7 minutes until opaque.
4. **Blanch Pea Pods:** Boil pea pods for 2-3 minutes until bright green but crisp. Drain and rinse under cold water to halt cooking.
5. **Mix Ingredients:** Combine the cooked perch and blanched pea pods in a bowl and toss gently.
6. **Serve:** Cool to room temperature before serving. Can be served alone or mixed with regular kibble.
7. **Storage:** Store leftovers in an airtight container in the refrigerator for up to 3 days.

TILAPIA AND BROCCOLI MOUSSE

Pureed steamed tilapia and broccoli, seasoned lightly with thyme

Protein: 65% | Fats: 20% | Carbohydrates: 10% | Minerals and vitamins: 5%

20 min	30 oz	450 (15 per oz) kcal

INGREDIENTS

- 18 oz tilapia fillets
- 12 oz fresh broccoli florets
- 1 tsp dried thyme
- Water for steaming

DIRECTIONS

1. **Prep Tilapia:** Inspect and debone tilapia fillets.
2. **Prep Broccoli:** Rinse broccoli florets.
3. **Steam Ingredients:** Place tilapia and broccoli in a steamer basket over boiling water. Cover and steam for 10-12 minutes until both are tender.
4. **Puree the Mixture:** Move the steamed tilapia and broccoli to a blender or food processor, add dried thyme, and puree until smooth. Thin with water or unsalted chicken broth if necessary.
5. **Cool and Serve:** Let the mousse cool to room temperature before serving.
6. **Storage:** Refrigerate leftovers in an airtight container for up to 3 days or freeze in portion-sized containers for up to a month.

SEA BASS AND PEA PUREE

Steamed sea bass blended into a fine puree with cooked peas

Protein: 70% | Fats: 20% | Carbohydrates: 8% | Minerals and vitamins: 2%

20 min	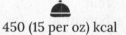 30 oz	450 (15 per oz) kcal

INGREDIENTS

- 20 oz sea bass fillets, deboned
- 10 oz green peas (fresh or frozen)
- Water for steaming

DIRECTIONS

1. **Prep Sea Bass:** Check sea bass fillets for bones, rinse under cold water, and pat dry.
2. **Steam Sea Bass and Peas:** Fill a steamer with water below the basket level. Add sea bass and peas, cover, and steam for 15 min until flaky and tender. For frozen peas, add in the last 5 min.
3. **Puree the Mixture:** Transfer cooked sea bass and peas to a blender. Blend into a smooth puree, adding steaming water or low-sodium broth if too thick.
4. **Cool and Serve:** Let the puree cool to room temperature before serving.
5. **Storage:** Refrigerate the puree in an airtight container for up to 3 days or freeze in portion-sized containers for up to a month.

SALMON AND PARSNIP PATTIES

Flaked salmon combined with mashed parsnip and a pinch of dill

Protein: 55% | Fats: 35% | Carbohydrates: 8% | Minerals and vitamins: 2%

30 min	32 oz	640 (20 per oz) kcal

INGREDIENTS

- 20 oz salmon fillets, cooked and flaked
- 10 oz parsnips, peeled, boiled, and mashed
- 2 oz fresh dill, finely chopped
- 1 egg (optional, helps bind the patties if cooking)

DIRECTIONS

1. **Cook Salmon:** Preheat the oven to 375°F (190°C). Bake the salmon fillets on a baking sheet for 15-20 min, let them cool, and then flake.
2. **Cook Parsnips:** Boil parsnip chunks until tender, about 15-20 min, then mash.
3. **Prep Dill:** Rinse and finely chop the dill.
4. **Mix Ingredients:** Combine flaked salmon, mashed parsnips, chopped dill, and an egg (optional) in a bowl and mix well.
5. **Form Patties:** Shape the mixture into half-inch thick patties.
6. **Cook Patties (Optional):** If cooking, fry patties in a lightly oiled pan over medium heat for 3-4 minutes on each side until golden.
7. **Cool and Serve:** Let patties cool to room temperature before serving.
8. **Storage:** Refrigerate in an airtight container for up to 3 days or freeze for up to a month.

GROUPER AND SWEET CORN MIX

Steamed grouper fillets flaked and mixed with cooked, mashed sweet corn

Protein: 60% | Fats: 25% | Carbohydrates: 10% | Minerals and vitamins: 5%

25 min	32 oz	640 (20 per oz) kcal

INGREDIENTS

- 20 oz grouper fillets
- 12 oz sweet corn, fresh or frozen
- Water for steaming

DIRECTIONS

1. **Prep Grouper Fillets:** Check for and remove any bones, then rinse under cold water.
2. **Sweet Corn:** Thaw completely if using frozen corn.
3. **Steam Grouper:** Fill a steamer with water below the basket, add the grouper, cover, and steam for 15-20 minutes until the fish flakes easily.
4. **Cook Sweet Corn:** For fresh corn, remove kernels from the cob and boil for 5-7 minutes until tender. For frozen, thawed corn, boil for 3-5 minutes. Drain and lightly mash the corn; a coarser texture is fine.
5. **Mix Ingredients:** Flake the grouper and combine it with the mashed corn in a large bowl.
6. **Cool and Serve:** Cool to room temperature before serving.
7. **Storage:** Refrigerate leftovers in an airtight container for up to 3 days or freeze for up to a month.

4.4. VEGETARIAN DISHES

4.4.1. The Benefits of Vegetarian Dishes in Your Dog's Diet

Introducing vegetarian dishes to your dog's diet can add a wonderful variety of flavors and nutrients that support their health and vitality. While dogs are naturally omnivorous, incorporating plant-based meals can offer some delightful benefits for your four-legged friend.

Here's why you might consider mixing in some vegetarian options:

• *Allergy-Friendly*: Some dogs are allergic to common protein sources like chicken, beef, or lamb. Vegetarian dishes can provide a safe and tasty alternative, helping you manage their allergies without sacrificing nutrition.

• *Gentle on the Stomach*: Plant-based ingredients are often more accessible on the digestive system, making them a great option for dogs with sensitive stomachs or those who need a lighter diet.

• *Rich in Fiber and Nutrients*: Vegetarian recipes are packed with fiber, which aids in digestion and keeps your dog feeling full and satisfied. Plus, they're loaded with essential vitamins and minerals that help maintain a healthy coat, strong bones, and overall vitality.

• *Low in Fat and Calories*: If you're keeping an eye on your dog's weight, vegetarian dishes are typically lower in fat and calories than meat-based options. This can help prevent obesity and support a healthy lifestyle, especially for less active dogs.

• *Variety is the Spice of Life*: Just like us, dogs enjoy a bit of variety in their meals. Introducing v egetarian options can spice up their diet and keep mealtime exciting.

• *Supports Hydration*: Many vegetarian dishes incorporate moisture-rich ingredients like cucumbers, zucchini, and tomatoes, which help keep your dog hydrated and their skin healthy.

When preparing vegetarian dishes for your dog, it is important to ensure a balanced diet. This means including a variety of vegetables, grains, and a supplementary protein source like eggs or dairy, if tolerated, to meet their nutritional needs. Always cook vegetables to make them more appealing and easier for your dog to digest.

4.4.2. Vegetarian Dishes Recipes

On the following pages, you will discover a variety of vegetarian recipes for your pet.

PUMPKIN RICE DELIGHT

Cooked brown rice mixed with pureed pumpkin and a sprinkle of parsley

Protein: 8% | Fat: 5% | Carbohydrates: 85% | Minerals and vitamins: 2%

45 min	🍽 32 oz	640 (20 per oz) kcal

INGREDIENTS

- 16 oz brown rice
- 12 oz pure pumpkin puree (ensure it's 100% pumpkin with no additives)
- 4 oz fresh parsley, finely chopped
- 4 cups water (for cooking rice)

DIRECTIONS

1. **Cook Brown Rice:** Rinse the rice under cold water until the water runs clear. In a medium pot, bring 4 cups of water to a boil. Add the rinsed rice, reduce heat to low, cover, and simmer for 30-35 minutes until the rice is tender and all the water has been absorbed.
2. **Prep Pumpkin Puree:** If using fresh pumpkin, peel, cube, and steam until tender, then blend into a puree. If using canned puree, ensure it's at room temperature.
3. **Chop Parsley:** Rinse and finely chop the fresh parsley.
4. **Mix Ingredients:** Combine the rice with the pumpkin puree and chopped parsley in a large mixing bowl. Stir thoroughly to ensure the pumpkin and parsley are evenly distributed throughout the rice.
5. **Cool Before Serving:** Allow the mixture to cool to room temperature before serving to ensure it's safe for your dog.

SWEET POTATO AND APPLE MASH

Boiled sweet potatoes and apples mashed together for a sweet and nutritious treat

Protein: 5% | Fat: 3% | Carbohydrates: 85% | Minerals and vitamins: 7%

🕐 30 min	🍽 32 oz	🍽 480 (15 per oz) kcal

INGREDIENTS

- 16 oz sweet potatoes, peeled and cubed
- 16 oz apples, cored and cubed (suitable varieties include Fuji, Gala, or Honeycrisp)
- Water for boiling

DIRECTIONS

1. **Prep Sweet Potatoes and Apples:** Peel and cube the sweet potatoes. Core and cube the apples, making sure to remove all seeds.
2. **Boil Sweet Potatoes:** Place the sweet potato cubes in a large pot and cover with water. Bring to a boil, then reduce heat to a simmer. Cook for about 20 minutes or until the sweet potatoes are very tender.
3. **Add Apples:** In the last 10 minutes of cooking, add the apple cubes to the pot with the sweet potatoes to soften them.
4. **Drain and Mash:** Once both the sweet potatoes and apples are soft, drain the water and return them to the pot. Use a potato masher or hand mixer to mash the mixture until smooth.
5. **Cool Before Serving:** Allow the mash to cool to room temperature before serving to ensure it's safe for your dog.

ZUCCHINI AND CARROT FRITTERS

Grated zucchini and carrots mixed with a bit of flaxseed meal

Protein: 10% | Fat: 15% | Carbohydrates: 70% | Minerals and vitamins: 5%

30 min	24 oz	480 (20 per oz) kcal

INGREDIENTS

- 12 oz zucchini, grated
- 12 oz carrots, grated
- 2 tbsps flaxseed meal
- 2 tbsps olive oil for frying

DIRECTIONS

1. **Prep Vegetables:** Wash and grate the zucchini and carrots. Use a clean cloth or paper towel to squeeze out moisture from the grated vegetables to ensure the fritters are not too soggy.
2. **Mix Ingredients:** Combine the grated zucchini, carrots, and flaxseed meal in a large bowl. Mix thoroughly.
3. **Shape Fritters:** Take small handfuls of the mixture and form them into patties about the size of a palm. If the mixture doesn't hold together well, you can add a little more flaxseed meal to help bind it.
4. **Fry the Fritters:** Heat the olive oil in a large skillet over medium heat. Add the fritters and cook for 3-4 minutes on each side or until golden brown and crispy.
5. **Cool Before Serving:** Transfer the fritters to a paper towel-lined plate to remove excess oil. Allow them to cool to room temperature.

GREEN BEAN AND COCONUT STEW

Chopped green beans cooked gently in coconut milk

Protein: 10% | Fat: 70% | Carbohydrates: 18% | Minerals and vitamins: 2%

25 min	30 oz	450 (15 per oz) kcal

INGREDIENTS

- 16 oz fresh green beans, trimmed and chopped
- 14 oz can of coconut milk (ensure it is unsweetened and free from additives)
- 1 tbsp coconut oil (for cooking)

DIRECTIONS

1. **Prep Green Beans:** Rinse the green beans under cold water, trim the ends, and chop them into bite-sized pieces.
2. **Heat Coconut Oil:** Heat the coconut oil over medium heat in a pot.
3. **Cook Green Beans:** Add the chopped green beans to the pot and sauté for 5 minutes until they soften.
4. **Add Coconut Milk:** Pour the coconut milk over the green beans and stir to combine.
5. **Simmer:** Reduce the heat to low and let the mixture simmer gently for 15-20 minutes, or until the green beans are tender and the stew thickens slightly.
6. **Cool Before Serving:** Allow the stew to cool to room temperature before serving to ensure it's safe for your dog.

BROCCOLI RICE CAKES

Chopped broccoli mixed with rice and formed into small cakes, then lightly fried

Protein: 10% | Fat: 15% | Carbohydrates: 70% | Minerals and vitamins: 5%

40 min

24 oz

480 (20 per oz) kcal

INGREDIENTS

- 12 oz cooked white rice, cooled
- 12 oz fresh broccoli, finely chopped
- 1 egg (to help bind the cakes)
- 2 tbsps olive oil (for frying)

DIRECTIONS

1. **Prep Ingredients:** Cook the rice according to the package instructions and let it cool. Rinse and finely chop the broccoli.
2. **Mix Ingredients:** In a large bowl, combine the cooled rice, chopped broccoli, and egg. Mix until the ingredients are well blended.
3. **Form Cakes:** Take small portions of the mixture and form them into small, flat cakes, about the size of a cookie.
4. **Heat Oil:** Heat olive oil in a large frying pan over medium heat.
5. **Cook Cakes:** Place the cakes in the frying pan and cook for 3-4 minutes on each side, or until golden brown and crispy.
6. **Cool Before Serving:** Remove the cakes from the pan and let them cool on a paper towel to absorb excess oil. Cool to room temperature.

BEET AND BERRY GEL

Pureed cooked beets mixed with blueberries and set with a little agar-agar

Protein: 5% | Fat: 5% | Carbohydrates: 85% | Minerals and vitamins: 5%

30 min

20 oz

400 (20 per oz) kcal

INGREDIENTS

- 10 oz beets, peeled and chopped
- 6 oz blueberries
- 4 oz water (for blending)
- 1 tsp agar-agar powder

DIRECTIONS

1. **Cook Beets:** Place the chopped beets in a pot, cover with water, and bring to a boil. Reduce heat and simmer until beets are tender, 15-20 minutes. Drain and let cool.
2. **Prep Berry Mixture:** Combine the cooked beets, blueberries, and 4 oz of water in a blender. Blend until smooth.
3. **Mix Agar-Agar:** Pour the pureed mixture into a saucepan. Sprinkle the agar-agar over the mixture and let it sit for 5 minutes.
4. **Heat and Stir:** Bring the mixture to a simmer over medium heat, stirring until the agar-agar is completely dissolved, 5-7 minutes.
5. **Set the Gel:** Pour the hot mixture into a mold or a shallow dish. Cool it at room temperature, then refrigerate until set, for 2 hours.
6. **Serve:** Once set, cut the gel into pieces appropriate for your dog.

CUCUMBER AND CARROT SALAD

Sliced cucumber and shredded carrot tossed with a bit of apple cider vinegar

Protein: 5% | Fat: 5% | Carbohydrates: 85% | Minerals and vitamins: 2%

10 min	20 oz	200 (10 per oz) kcal

INGREDIENTS

- 10 oz cucumbers, thinly sliced
- 10 oz carrots, peeled and shredded
- 1 tbsp apple cider vinegar

DIRECTIONS

1. **Prep Vegetables:** Rinse the cucumbers and thinly slice them. Peel the carrots and shred them using a grater or food processor.
2. **Toss with Vinegar:** In a large mixing bowl, combine the sliced cucumbers and shredded carrots. Drizzle with apple cider vinegar and gently toss the vegetables to coat evenly.
3. **Chill Before Serving:** Refrigerate the salad for 5 minutes to enhance the flavors and provide a cooling effect, making it a refreshing treat.
4. **Serve:** Allow the salad to come to room temperature before serving to your dog

SPINACH AND CHICKPEA SCOOPS

Cooked chickpeas mixed with chopped spinach, and baked

Protein: 20% | Fat: 15% | Carbohydrates: 60% | Minerals and vitamins: 5%

40 min	16 oz	 600 (37.5 per oz) kcal

INGREDIENTS

- 2 cups cooked chickpeas (approximately 1 cup dry)
- 2 cups fresh spinach, finely chopped
- 1 tbsp olive oil
- 1 egg (for binding)

DIRECTIONS

1. **Preheat Oven:** Set your oven to 375°F (190°C).
2. **Prep Ingredients:** If using dry chickpeas, soak them overnight and cook until tender. Drain well.
3. **Mash Chickpeas:** In a large bowl, mash the cooked chickpeas with a fork or potato masher until mostly smooth.
4. **Mix Ingredients:** Add the chopped spinach, olive oil, and egg to the mashed chickpeas. Stir until all ingredients are well combined.
5. **Shape Scoops:** Form the mixture into small balls, about 1 inch in diameter.
6. **Bake:** Place the scoops on a baking sheet lined with parchment paper. Bake in the preheated oven for 25 minutes.
7. **Cool:** Allow the scoops to cool before serving to your dog.

OAT AND BANANA MINI MUFFINS

Sliced cucumber and shredded carrot tossed with a bit of apple cider vinegar

Protein: 10% | Fat: 15% | Carbohydrates: 70% | Minerals and vitamins: 5%

30 min	24 oz	480 (20 per oz) kcal

INGREDIENTS

- 8 oz rolled oats
- 8 oz ripe bananas (about 2 medium bananas), mashed
- 1 tsp cinnamon
- 8 oz water or unsweetened almond milk

DIRECTIONS

1. **Preheat Oven:** Preheat your oven to 350°F (175°C).
2. **Prep the Mixture:** In a large bowl, mix the mashed bananas with the rolled oats. Add the cinnamon and water or almond milk to create a moist, well-combined batter.
3. **Prep Muffin Pan:** Grease a mini muffin pan with a small amount of olive oil or use silicone muffin cups to prevent sticking.
4. **Fill Muffin Cups:** Spoon the mixture into the mini muffin cups, filling each cup about three-quarters full to allow for some rising.
5. **Bake:** Place the muffin pan in the preheated oven and bake for 15-20 minutes, or until a toothpick inserted into the center of a muffin comes out clean.
6. **Cool Muffins:** Let them cool briefly in the pan, then transfer to a wire rack to finish cooling.
7. **Serve:** Ensure the muffins are at room temperature before serving to your dog.

CELERY AND PEANUT BUTTER CRUNCH

Chopped celery mixed with peanut butter and formed into bite-size treats

Protein: 25% | Fat: 65% | Carbohydrates: 8% | Minerals and vitamins: 2%

10 min	20 oz	600 (30 per oz) kcal

INGREDIENTS

- 10 oz celery, finely chopped
- 10 oz unsweetened peanut butter (make sure it does not contain xylitol, which is toxic to dogs)
- Optional: 1 tsp flaxseed for extra omega-3 fatty acids

DIRECTIONS

1. **Prep Ingredients:** Rinse and finely chop the celery into small pieces suitable for your dog's size. If using flaxseed, grind it into a fine powder using a coffee grinder or food processor.
2. **Mix Ingredients:** Combine the chopped celery with unsweetened peanut butter in a medium-sized bowl. If adding flaxseed, mix it in currently. Stir until all ingredients are evenly distributed.
3. **Form Treats:** Scoop small amounts of the mixture and roll into bite-sized balls or small logs. Place these on a baking sheet lined with parchment paper.
4. **Chill to Set:** Place the baking sheet in the refrigerator for at least 1 hour to allow the treats to firm up and hold their shape.
5. **Serve:** The treats can be served to your dog once firm.

PEAR AND PARSNIP PUREE

Steamed pears and parsnips blended into a smooth puree

Protein: 5% | Fats: 5% | Carbohydrates: 85% | Minerals and vitamins: 5%

25 min	20 oz	400 (20 per oz) kcal

INGREDIENTS

- 10 oz pears, peeled, cored, and chopped
- 10 oz parsnips, peeled and chopped
- Water for steaming

DIRECTIONS

1. **Prep Ingredients:** Peel the pears and parsnips. Core the pears and chop both the pears and parsnips into small, even.
2. **Steam Ingredients:** Place the chopped pears and parsnips in a steaming basket over a pot of boiling water. Cover and steam for 15-20 minutes until both are very tender.
3. **Blend to Puree:** Transfer the steamed pears and parsnips to a blender or food processor. Blend until smooth, adding a small amount of water if necessary to achieve the desired consistency.
4. **Cool and Serve:** To ensure it is safe for your dog, allow the puree to cool completely before serving. You can store this puree in the refrigerator for up to 3 days or freeze it in ice cube trays for easy portioning later.

MUSHROOM AND RICE STUFFED PEPPERS

Bell peppers stuffed with a mixture of sautéed mushrooms and cooked rice

Protein: 10% | Fats: 15% | Carbohydrates: 70% | Minerals and vitamins: 5%

45 min	30 oz	450 (15 per oz) kcal

INGREDIENTS

- 4 large bell peppers (about 24 oz total)
- 8 oz mushrooms, finely chopped
- 6 oz cooked white or brown rice
- 2 tbsps olive oil
- Water for steaming

DIRECTIONS

1. **Prep the Bell Peppers:** Wash the peppers, cut off the tops, and remove the seeds. Set aside the tops.
2. **Cook the Rice:** Cook the rice according to the package instructions. You can use white or brown rice, as you prefer.
3. **Sauté Mushrooms:** Heat the olive oil in a skillet over medium heat. Add the mushrooms and sauté until they are soft, about 5-7 min.
4. **Combine the Filling:** Mix the rice and mushrooms in a bowl.
5. **Stuff the Peppers:** Fill the hollowed-out bell peppers with the mushroom and rice mixture, lightly packing to ensure a complete fill.
6. **Cook the Peppers:** Place the stuffed peppers in a baking dish and add water (1/4 in) to steam them.
7. **Bake:** Heat the oven to 375°F (190°C). Cover the peppers with foil and bake for 30 minutes. Remove the foil and bake for 10-15 minutes until the peppers are tender and lightly browned.
8. **Cool and Serve:** Let the peppers cool to a safe temperature before serving them to your dog.

APPLE AND OAT CRISP

Layered slices of apple and oats, sprinkled with cinnamon and baked until crisp

Protein: 10% | Fats: 15% | Carbohydrates: 70% | Minerals and vitamins: 5%

45 min	24 oz	480 (20 per oz) kcal

INGREDIENTS

- 12 oz apples, cored and thinly sliced
- 8 oz rolled oats
- 4 oz water
- 1 tsp cinnamon

DIRECTIONS

1. **Preheat Oven:** Set your oven to 350°F (175°C).
2. **Prep Apples:** Wash the apples and core and cut them into thin slices.
3. **Mix Oats and Cinnamon:** In a bowl, mix the rolled oats with cinnamon to distribute the spice evenly.
4. **Layer Ingredients:** Layer half of the apple slices at the bottom in a baking dish. Sprinkle half of the oat mixture over the apples. Repeat with the remaining apples and oats to create another set of layers.
5. **Add Water:** Evenly pour the water over the layered mixture. It will create steam, which will cook the apples and oats thoroughly.
6. **Bake:** Cover the baking dish with foil and bake in the oven for 35 minutes. Then remove the foil and bake for 10 minutes to crisp up the top.
7. **Cool and Serve:** Cool the meal before serving to your dog.

CARROT AND PEA CRUNCHIES

Carrots and peas mashed and shaped into small patties, then baked

Protein: 20% | Fats: 10% | Carbohydrates: 65% | Minerals and vitamins: 5%

50 min	20 oz	300 (15 per oz) kcal

INGREDIENTS

- 10 oz carrots, peeled and chopped
- 10 oz peas (fresh or frozen)
- Water for steaming
- Optional: 1 tbsp olive oil for binding and extra flavor

DIRECTIONS

1. **Preheat Oven:** Set your oven to 375°F (190°C).
2. **Steam Vegetables:** Place the chopped carrots and peas in a steamer over boiling water. Cover and steam for 10-15 minutes.
3. **Mash Vegetables:** Transfer the steamed carrots and peas to a large bowl. Mash them together until mostly smooth. If desired, stir in a tbsp of olive oil to help bind the mixture and add a bit of healthy fat.
4. **Shape Patties:** Once the vegetable mixture has cooled enough to handle, shape it into small, flat patties, about 2 inches in diameter.
5. **Bake Patties:** Line a baking sheet with parchment paper and place the patties on the sheet. Bake in the preheated oven for 20-25 minutes or until the edges are golden and the patties are firm.
6. **Cool and Serve:** Allow the patties to cool completely on a cooling rack before serving to ensure they are safe for your dog to eat.

BUTTERNUT SQUASH BITES

Cubed butternut squash baked with a sprinkle of thyme until soft.

Protein: 5% | Fats: 5% | Carbohydrates: 85% | Minerals and vitamins: 5%

30 min	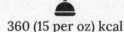 24 oz	360 (15 per oz) kcal

INGREDIENTS

- 24 oz butternut squash, peeled, seeded, and cubed
- 1 tsp dried thyme
- 1 tbsp olive oil (optional, to help coat the squash and herbs)

DIRECTIONS

1. **Preheat Oven:** Set your oven to 375°F (190°C).
2. **Prep Squash:** Peel the butternut squash, remove the seeds, and cut it into small, bite-sized cubes.
3. **Season Squash:** Toss the butternut squash cubes with the dried thyme in a large mixing bowl. If using, drizzle with olive oil to help the thyme adhere and add a bit of healthy fat to the dish.
4. **Arrange on Baking Sheet:** Spread the squash cubes on a baking sheet in a single layer, ensuring they do not overlap.
5. **Bake:** Place the baking sheet in the preheated oven and bake for 25-30 minutes, or until the squash is soft and the edges start to turn golden brown.
6. **Cool Before Serving:** Let the meal cool completely before serving.

SWEET POTATO AND LENTIL LOAF

Hearty loaf blending sweet potatoes and lentils

Protein: 15% | Fats: 10% | Carbohydrates: 70% | Minerals and vitamins: 5%

1 h	40 oz	800 (20 per oz) kcal

INGREDIENTS

- 16 oz sweet potatoes, peeled and cubed
- 12 oz cooked lentils
- 4 oz peas
- 4 oz carrots, finely chopped
- 2 eggs
- 2 tbsps olive oil
- 1 tsp dried parsley

DIRECTIONS

1. **Preheat Oven:** Set your oven to 375°F (190°C).
2. **Prep Sweet Potatoes:** Boil them in water until tender, 15-20 minutes. Drain and mash.
3. **Cook Lentils:** If not using pre-cooked lentils, rinse 1/2 cup of dry lentils and boil in water for 20 minutes until soft.
4. **Mix Ingredients:** In a large bowl, combine and mix the mashed sweet potatoes, cooked lentils, peas, chopped carrots, eggs, olive oil, and parsley.
5. **Shape Loaf:** Transfer the mixture to a greased loaf pan, smoothing the top with a spoon.
6. **Bake:** Place the loaf in the preheated oven and bake for 40 minutes, or until the top is golden and a toothpick inserted into the center comes out clean.
7. **Cool and Serve:** Let the loaf cool in the pan for 10 minutes, then remove and slice. Ensure the loaf is completely cool before serving to your dog.

VEGAN DOGGIE STEW

Stew with sweet potatoes, carrots, green beans, peas, pumpkin

Protein: 10% | Fats: 5% | Carbohydrates: 80% | Minerals and vitamins: 5%

45 min	40 oz	400 (10 per oz) kcal

INGREDIENTS

- 8 oz sweet potatoes, peeled and cubed
- 8 oz carrots, peeled and sliced
- 8 oz green beans, trimmed and cut into pieces
- 8 oz peas (fresh or frozen)
- 8 oz pumpkin, peeled and cubed
- 4 cups water or vegetable broth (ensure no onions or garlic in the broth)
- 1 tsp turmeric
- 1 tbsp parsley, finely chopped

DIRECTIONS

1. **Prep Ingredients**: Wash and peel all vegetables. Cut sweet potatoes, carrots, and pumpkin into small, bite-sized cubes. Slice the green beans.
2. **Cook Stew**: Combine all the vegetables in a large pot, cover with water or vegetable broth, and bring to a boil.
3. **Add Spices**: Once boiling, reduce heat to a simmer and add turmeric and parsley. Stir well.
4. **Simmer**: Cover the pot and let simmer for 30-35 minutes until all vegetables are tender.
5. **Cool and Serve**: Allow the stew to cool to room temperature before serving to ensure it's safe for your dog.

QUINOA AND CARROT BALLS

Bite-sized quinoa and carrot treats

Protein: 15% | Fats: 10% | Carbohydrates: 70% | Minerals and vitamins: 5%

 30 min	35 oz	450 (15 per oz) kcal

INGREDIENTS

- 12 oz cooked quinoa (about 1 cup uncooked)
- 10 oz carrots, finely grated
- 4 oz peas (fresh or frozen)
- 2 eggs, beaten
- 2 tbsps parsley, finely chopped
- 1 tbsps olive oil (for greasing the baking sheet)

DIRECTIONS

1. **Preheat Oven**: Set your oven to 350°F (175°C).
2. **Prep Quinoa**: Rinse 1 cup of quinoa under cold water, combine with 2 cups of water, bring to a boil, then simmer covered for 15 minutes until the water is absorbed.
3. **Mix Ingredients**: In a large bowl, combine the cooked quinoa, grated carrots, peas, beaten eggs, and chopped parsley. Mix thoroughly to ensure the ingredients are evenly distributed.
4. **Shape Balls**: Form the mixture into small balls, about 1 inch in diameter. Place them on a greased or lined baking sheet.
5. **Bake**: Bake in the preheated oven for 20-25 minutes or until the balls are firm and slightly golden outside.
6. **Cool and Serve**: Let the quinoa and carrot balls cool fully before serving. Store them in an airtight container in the fridge.

CAULIFLOWER AND SPINACH MASH

Smooth mix of cauliflower and spinach

Protein: 10% | Fats: 10% | Carbohydrates: 75% | Minerals and vitamins: 5%

25 min	24 oz	240 (10 per oz) kcal

INGREDIENTS

- 16 oz cauliflower, cut into florets
- 8 oz fresh spinach
- 1 tbsp coconut oil

DIRECTIONS

1. **Prep Cauliflower:** Rinse the cauliflower florets under cold water. Place them in a steaming basket over boiling water and steam for 10-15 minutes or until they are very tender.
2. **Add Spinach:** In the last 5 minutes of steaming the cauliflower, add the spinach to the steamer to wilt.
3. **Mash the Vegetables:** Place steamed cauliflower and spinach in a bowl, and add coconut oil for better texture and health benefits. Mash or blend until smooth; use a food processor for a finer consistency.
4. **Cool and Serve:** Allow the mash to cool completely before serving to ensure it is safe for your dog.

LENTIL VEGGIE STEW

Simple, filling stew with lentils and vegetables

Protein: 20% | Fats: 5% | Carbohydrates: 70% | Minerals and vitamins: 5%

45 min	40 oz	600 (15 per oz) kcal

INGREDIENTS

- 12 oz lentils, rinsed
- 8 oz carrots, diced
- 8 oz potatoes, diced
- 4 oz green beans, chopped
- 4 oz peas
- 4 cups water or low-sodium vegetable broth (ensure it's onion- and garlic-free)
- 1 tsp turmeric (optional for added health benefits)

DIRECTIONS

1. **Prep Ingredients:** Wash and dice the carrots and potatoes. Chop the green beans into bite-sized pieces.
2. **Cook Lentils:** Add the rinsed lentils and water or vegetable broth to a large pot. Bring to a boil over high heat, then reduce to a simmer.
3. **Add Vegetables:** Once the lentils have softened (about 15 minutes), add the carrots, potatoes, green beans, and peas to the pot. Stir in the turmeric if using.
4. **Simmer:** Simmer the stew for another 30 minutes or until the lentils are fully cooked and the vegetables are tender.
5. **Cool and Serve:** Let the stew cool before serving. Store in the refrigerator for up to 5 days or freeze for extended storage.

4.5. RAW MIX DISHES

4.5.1. Importance of Raw Mix Dishes in a Dog's Diet

In the quest for optimal canine health, the inclusion of raw mix dishes in a dog's diet plays a pivotal role. Raw mix dishes, which typically consist of raw meats, bones, vegetables, and fruits, can offer various nutritional benefits often diminished in cooked foods.

Here's why you might consider mixing in some vegetarian options:

• *Enhanced Nutrient Absorption:* Raw mix dishes provide nutrients in their most natural and accessible form. Unlike cooked dishes, raw foods preserve their vitamins, enzymes, and natural probiotics, which are crucial for a dog's digestive health. The body readily absorbs and utilizes these nutrients, promoting better digestion and nutrient assimilation.

• *Natural Enzymes:* The natural enzymes found in raw foods help aid digestion, allowing dogs to break down their food more efficiently. This can improve gastrointestinal health, fewer digestive disorders, and better overall wellness.

• *Dental Health:* Raw bones and some of the tougher, fibrous plant materials in raw dishes can act as natural toothbrushes, scrubbing away plaque from your dog's teeth. Chewing raw bones also helps to strengthen gums and reduce the risk of dental issues such as gum disease and tooth decay.

• *Allergy Mitigation:* Many dogs suffer from allergies related to processed foods. Raw mix dishes, free from artificial additives, preservatives, and fillers, reduce the risk of food-related allergic reactions. By sticking to a diet closer to what their ancestors would have eaten, many dogs experience fewer allergy symptoms.

• *Weight Management:* Raw diets can be particularly beneficial in managing a dog's weight. They are typically more satisfying than processed foods, leading to less overeating. Raw diets' high protein and moderate fat content help maintain lean muscle mass while reducing excess body fat.

• *Energy and Vitality:* Dogs fed a raw diet often show increased energy levels and vitality. The nutritional richness of raw food means that dogs can utilize more of what they eat, which translates into better stamina and overall health.

• *Tailoring to Specific Needs:* Raw mix dishes can be easily customized to suit the specific health needs of a dog, such as adjusting the types of meat, or vegetables used based on allergies, age, or health conditions.

Considerations

While the benefits of raw mix dishes are significant, it's crucial to approach this diet with care:

• *Balance:* Ensure that the diet is balanced with the correct proportions of protein, fat, and carbohydrates, as well as essential vitamins and minerals.

• *Hygiene:* Raw diets require strict hygiene practices to prevent bacterial contamination.

• **Transition:** If transitioning from a cooked to a raw diet, do so gradually to allow your dog's digestive system to adjust.

• **Consultation with a Vet:** Always discuss dietary changes with your veterinarian, especially when it involves raw food, to ensure it fits your dog's specific health profile.

Incorporating raw mix dishes into your dog's diet can be a pathway to enhanced health and vitality. With careful planning and consideration, a raw diet can provide a wholesome, satisfying, and nutritionally rich meal plan that your dog will thrive on.

4.5.2. Raw Mix Dishes Recipes

On the following pages, you will find dishes for your furry friend made from raw ingredients. Please approach these dishes cautiously, introduce them gradually, and consult with your dog's veterinarian who can assist in selecting such meals based on your pet's health and other specific characteristics.

CHICKEN AND APPLE RAW MIX

Chopped raw chicken breast mixed with grated apple and chopped mint

Protein: 60% | Fat: 20% | Carbohydrates: 15% | Minerals and vitamins: 5%

10 min	24 oz	480 (20 per oz) kcal

INGREDIENTS

- 16 oz raw chicken breast, finely chopped
- 8 oz apple (e.g., Fuji or Gala), cored and grated
- 1 tbsp fresh mint, finely chopped
- Optional: 1 tsp of coconut oil for added healthy fats

DIRECTIONS

1. **Prep Chicken:** Thoroughly wash the chicken breast and pat it dry. Finely chop it into small, bite-sized pieces. Ensure there are no bones or tough pieces.
2. **Prep Apple:** Wash, core, and grate the apple. If desired, toss the grated apple in a little lemon juice to prevent browning.
3. **Chop Mint:** Wash and finely chop the fresh mint leaves.
4. **Mix Ingredients:** In a large bowl, combine the finely chopped chicken, grated apple, and chopped mint. If using coconut oil, mix it in currently to enhance the fat content and palatability.
5. **Serve:** Once mixed, the raw food can be served immediately or stored in the refrigerator.

TURKEY AND BLUEBERRY DELIGHT

Ground raw turkey with mashed blueberries and plain yogurt

Protein: 55% | Fat: 30% | Carbohydrates: 10% | Minerals and vitamins: 5%

15 min	32 oz	640 (20 per oz) kcal

INGREDIENTS

- 24 oz ground raw turkey
- 6 oz blueberries, fresh or frozen (if frozen, thaw first)
- 2 oz plain yogurt (ensure it is non-fat and does not contain xylitol or artificial sweeteners)

DIRECTIONS

1. **Prep Turkey:** Ensure the raw turkey is fresh and sourced from a reputable supplier. Place it in a large mixing bowl.
2. **Mash Blueberries:** Mash the blueberries in a separate bowl using a fork or a blender until you achieve a rough puree. If using frozen blueberries, ensure they are fully thawed to mash them properly.
3. **Mix Ingredients:** Add the mashed blueberries and plain yogurt to the bowl with the ground turkey. Mix thoroughly.
4. **Portion the Mixture:** If you wish to use this as a meal prep, portion the mixture into daily serving sizes based on your dog's weight and caloric needs.
5. **Serve:** You can serve this mixture immediately or store it in the refrigerator in airtight containers for up to 48 hours.

DUCK AND CRANBERRY COMBO

Ground raw duck mixed with crushed cranberries

Protein: 50% | Fat: 45% | Carbohydrates: 3% | Minerals and vitamins: 2%

| 20 min | 32 oz | 960 (30 per oz) kcal |

INGREDIENTS

- 24 oz raw duck, ground
- 6 oz fresh cranberries, crushed
- 2 oz fresh parsley, finely chopped
- Optional: 1 tsp fish oil for additional omega-3 fatty acids

DIRECTIONS

1. **Prepare Duck:** Ensure the duck meat is fresh and sourced from a reputable supplier. Ground the duck if not already purchased ground. Keep refrigerated until use.
2. **Crush Cranberries:** Rinse the cranberries and crush them using a food processor or manually with a muddler or the back of a spoon to release their juices.
3. **Chop Parsley:** Wash and finely chop the parsley.
4. **Mix Ingredients:** In a large bowl, combine the ground duck, crushed cranberries, chopped parsley, and fish oil if using. Mix thoroughly to ensure even distribution of the ingredients.
5. **Serve Fresh:** This meal is best served fresh. Portion the mixture according to your dog's size and serve immediately.

BEEF AND CARROT TARTARE

Minced raw beef with grated carrots

Protein: 60% | Fat: 35% | Carbohydrates: 3% | Minerals and vitamins: 2%

| 15 min | 24 oz | 720 (30 per oz) kcal |

INGREDIENTS

- 18 oz raw beef (choose a lean cut like top round or sirloin), minced
- 6 oz carrots, peeled and grated
- 1 tbsp olive oil

DIRECTIONS

1. **Prep Beef:** Ensure the beef is fresh and sourced from a reputable butcher. Trim any excess fat and mince the beef finely. It is crucial to keep the beef chilled until ready to use to prevent bacterial growth.
2. **Prep Carrots:** Wash, peel, and grate the carrots using a fine grater.
3. **Mix Ingredients:** In a large mixing bowl, combine the minced beef, grated carrots, and olive oil. Mix thoroughly to ensure even distribution of the ingredients.
4. **Serve Immediately:** To maintain freshness, serve the tartare immediately or cover and refrigerate for up to 12 hours.

SALMON AND SPINACH MEDLEY

Finely chopped raw salmon mixed with shredde

Protein: 55% | Fat: 40% | Carbohydrates: 3% | Minerals and vitamins: 2%

10 min	24 oz	🍽 720 (30 per oz) kcal

INGREDIENTS

- 16 oz raw salmon, finely chopped
- 6 oz fresh spinach, shredded
- 2 oz flaxseed oil

DIRECTIONS

1. **Prep Salmon:** Ensure the salmon is fresh and of high quality. Remove any bones and skin, then finely chop the salmon into small, bite-sized pieces.
2. **Prep Spinach:** Wash the spinach thoroughly, then shred it into fine strips. This can be done with a knife or a food processor for a finer texture.
3. **Mix Ingredients:** In a large bowl, combine the finely chopped salmon with the shredded spinach. Drizzle the flaxseed oil over the mixture and toss gently to ensure everything is evenly coated.
4. **Serve:** The Salmon and Spinach Medley can be served immediately or refrigerated for up to 24 hours if needed.

PORK AND PEA SNAP

Minced raw pork with finely chopped sugar snap peas

Protein: 50% | Fat: 45% | Carbohydrates: 4% | Minerals and vitamins: 1%

20 min	🌀 32 oz	🍽 960 (30 per oz) kcal

INGREDIENTS

- 24 oz raw pork, minced (choose lean cuts to minimize fat)
- 6 oz sugar snap peas, finely chopped
- 2 oz coconut oil

DIRECTIONS

1. **Prep Pork:** Source high-quality, lean pork from a reputable butcher. Ensure it is fresh and minced. If not pre-minced, chop it finely with a sharp knife or in a food processor.
2. **Chop Sugar Snap Peas:** Wash the sugar snap peas thoroughly. Remove the stem ends and strings, then finely chop them to ensure they are digestible and safe for your dog.
3. **Mix Ingredients:** In a large mixing bowl, combine the minced pork, chopped sugar snap peas, and coconut oil. Stir thoroughly until all components are evenly distributed.
4. **Portion and Serve:** Portion the mixture based on your dog's size and caloric needs. This meal can be served immediately or stored in the refrigerator for short-term use.

CHICKEN LIVER AND ZUCCHINI PLATE

Chopped raw chicken liver with grated zucchini and salmon oil

Protein: 50% | Fat: 35% | Carbohydrates: 10% | Minerals and vitamins: 5%

20 min	32 oz	640 (20 per oz) kcal

INGREDIENTS

- 20 oz raw chicken liver, finely chopped
- 10 oz zucchini, grated
- 2 oz salmon oil

DIRECTIONS

1. **Prep Chicken Liver:** Rinse the chicken liver under cold water and pat dry. Chop it finely into small, bite-sized pieces.
2. **Grate Zucchini:** Wash the zucchini thoroughly. Grate it using a fine grater or food processor. Ensure no large chunks remain, as finely grated zucchini is easier for dogs to digest.
3. **Mix Ingredients:** In a large mixing bowl, combine the chopped chicken liver, grated zucchini, and salmon oil. Mix thoroughly until all ingredients are evenly distributed.
4. **Portion and Serve:** Portion the mixture based on your dog's size and caloric needs. Serve immediately or store in the refrigerator for up to 24 hours.

LAMB AND CUCUMBER MIX

Chopped raw lamb with diced cucumber and a sprinkle of dill

Protein: 55% | Fat: 40% | Carbohydrates: 3% | Minerals and vitamins: 2%

20 min	32 oz	960 (30 per oz) kcal

INGREDIENTS

- 20 oz raw lamb, finely chopped
- 10 oz cucumber, peeled and diced
- 2 oz fresh dill, finely chopped

DIRECTIONS

1. **Prep Lamb:** Ensure the lamb is fresh and sourced from a reputable supplier. Finely chop it into small, bite-sized pieces. Keep refrigerated until ready to use.
2. **Prep Cucumber:** Wash and peel the cucumber, then dice it into small cubes.
3. **Chop Dill:** Wash and finely chop the fresh dill.
4. **Mix Ingredients:** In a large mixing bowl, combine the chopped lamb, diced cucumber, and chopped dill. Mix thoroughly until all ingredients are evenly distributed.
5. **Portion and Serve:** Portion the mixture based on your dog's size and caloric needs. Serve immediately or store in the refrigerator for up to 24 hours.

VENISON AND SWEET POTATO HASH

Minced raw venison mixed with grated sweet potato and a touch of turmeric

Protein: 55% | Fats: 30% | Carbohydrates: 10% | Minerals and vitamins: 5%

| 15 min | 32 oz | 640 (20 per oz) kcal |

INGREDIENTS

- 16 oz raw venison, minced
- 14 oz sweet potatoes, peeled and grated
- 2 oz coconut oil
- 1 tsp turmeric powder

DIRECTIONS

1. **Prep Venison:** Finely chop the raw venison, ensuring it is free from bones and any tough connective tissue.
2. **Prep Sweet Potatoes:** Peel and grate the sweet potatoes.
3. **Mix Ingredients:** In a large bowl, combine the minced venison, grated sweet potatoes, coconut oil, and turmeric. Mix thoroughly.
4. **Raw Serving Option:** If your dog is accustomed to a raw diet, you can serve this mixture raw. Ensure it is fresh and handle it with strict hygiene.
5. **Cooked Serving Option:** If you prefer to cook the hash, spread the mixture on a baking tray and bake in an oven at 350°F (175°C) for 20 minutes or until the venison is thoroughly cooked.
6. **Serving:** Cool the hash to room temperature before serving.

RABBIT AND KALE BLEND

Ground raw rabbit mixed with chopped kale and a few cranberries.

Protein: 60% | Fats: 30% | Carbohydrates: 5% | Minerals and vitamins: 5%

| 20 min | 32 oz | 640 (20 per oz) kcal |

INGREDIENTS

- 20 oz raw rabbit meat, ground
- 10 oz kale, finely chopped
- 2 oz cranberries, fresh or unsweetened dried, chopped

DIRECTIONS

1. **Prep Rabbit:** You can grind the rabbit meat yourself or have your butcher do it, removing all bones.
2. **Prep Kale:** Wash and finely chop the kale for easy digestion.
3. **Prep Cranberries:** Rinse and finely chop fresh cranberries or check dried cranberries to ensure they are unsweetened before chopping.
4. **Mix Ingredients:** Combine ground rabbit, kale, and cranberries in a bowl and mix well.
5. **Serve or Store:** Serve the blend at room temperature, store it in airtight containers in the fridge for up to 3 days, or freeze it for later use.

QUAIL AND PUMPKIN SEED MIX

Ground raw quail mixed with crushed pumpkin seeds and diced apple.

Protein: 55% | Fats: 35% | Carbohydrates: 5% | Minerals and vitamins: 5%

 20 min |  32 oz | 640 (20 per oz) kcal

INGREDIENTS

- 20 oz raw quail meat, ground
- 8 oz pumpkin seeds, crushed
- 4 oz apples, cored and diced

DIRECTIONS

1. **Prep Quail:** Grind quail meat, ensuring bones are finely ground to avoid choking hazards.
2. **Crush Pumpkin Seeds:** Lightly crush pumpkin seeds using a mortar and pestle or food processor; they should be broken into small pieces.
3. **Prep Apple:** Core and dice the apple into small, dog-size appropriate pieces.
4. **Mix Ingredients:** Combine ground quail, crushed pumpkin seeds, and diced apple in a large bowl, mixing well.
5. **Serve or Store:** Serve fresh or portion into meal-sized servings and store in airtight containers. Refrigerate for up to 3 days or freeze for up to a month.

BISON AND BEET MIX

Minced raw bison with grated beetroot and a sprinkle of ground flax seeds

Protein: 55% | Fats: 35% | Carbohydrates: 5% | Minerals and vitamins: 5%

 20 min | 32 oz | 640 (20 per oz) kcal

INGREDIENTS

- 20 oz raw bison meat, minced
- 10 oz beetroot, peeled and grated
- 2 oz ground flax seeds

DIRECTIONS

1. **Prep Bison:** To guarantee freshness, ensure the bison meat is sourced from a reputable supplier. Mince the meat finely or purchase pre-minced bison.
2. **Prep Beetroot:** Peel the beetroot and grate it using a medium grater. Wear gloves to avoid staining your hands.
3. **Mix Ingredients:** In a large bowl, combine the minced bison, grated beetroot, and ground flax seeds. Mix thoroughly to ensure even distribution of all ingredients.
4. **Serve or Store:** This blend can be served immediately or portioned into meal-sized servings and stored. For storage, place in airtight containers and refrigerate for up to 2 days or freeze for up to a month.

FISH TRIO TARTARE

Mix of chopped raw salmon, trout, and sardines with chopped parsley and olive oil

Protein: 60% | Fats: 35% | Carbohydrates: 2% | Minerals and vitamins: 3%

15 min	30 oz	600 (20 per oz) kcal

INGREDIENTS

- 10 oz raw salmon, finely chopped
- 10 oz raw trout, finely chopped
- 10 oz raw sardines, finely chopped
- 2 tbsps chopped parsley
- 2 tbsps olive oil

DIRECTIONS

1. **Prep Fish:** Start by ensuring all fish is fresh and sourced from reputable suppliers. Remove any bones carefully, then finely chop the salmon, trout, and sardines into small, bite-sized pieces suitable for your dog.
2. **Chop Parsley:** Wash and finely chop fresh parsley. Parsley is great for freshening breath and providing essential vitamins.
3. **Mix Ingredients:** Combine the chopped fish with the parsley and olive oil in a large mixing bowl. Please make sure all ingredients are evenly coated and mixed.
4. **Serve or Store:** This tartare can be served fresh or divided into meal-sized portions and stored. For storage, place in airtight containers and refrigerate for up to 2 days or freeze for up to a month.

TURKEY AND BROCCOLI RABE

Ground raw turkey with finely chopped broccoli rabe and a few drops of hemp oil

Protein: 55% | Fats: 30% | Carbohydrates: 10% | Minerals and vitamins: 5%

20 min	32 oz	480 (15 per oz) kcal

INGREDIENTS

- 20 oz raw turkey, ground
- 10 oz broccoli rabe, finely chopped
- 2 tbsps hemp oil

DIRECTIONS

1. **Prep Turkey:** If the turkey isn't pre-ground, grind the turkey using a meat grinder. Ensure it is fresh and handled hygienically.
2. **Prep Broccoli Rabe:** Rinse the broccoli rabe thoroughly to remove any dirt or chemicals. Chop it finely to ensure it is easily digestible for your dog.
3. **Mix Ingredients:** In a large bowl, combine the ground turkey, finely chopped broccoli rabe, and hemp oil. Mix thoroughly to ensure the hemp oil evenly coats the mixture.
4. **Serve or Store:** This meal can be served immediately or portioned into meal-sized servings and stored. For storage, place in airtight containers and refrigerate for up to 2 days or freeze for up to a month.

SARDINE AND SWEET PEA MASH

Mashed raw sardines mixed with crushed sweet peas and a hint of rosemary

Protein: 60% | Fats: 30% | Carbohydrates: 8% | Minerals and vitamins: 2%

 15 min   32 oz   640 (20 per oz) kcal

INGREDIENTS

- 20 oz raw sardines, cleaned and deboned
- 10 oz fresh or frozen sweet peas, if frozen, thawed
- 2 oz fresh rosemary, finely chopped
- Optional: 1 tbsp olive oil for additional healthy fats

DIRECTIONS

1. **Prep Sardines:** Ensure sardines are fresh. Remove all bones carefully to prevent any choking hazards. Mash the sardines using a fork or food processor until they reach a paste-like consistency.
2. **Prep Sweet Peas:** If using frozen peas, ensure they are fully thawed. Mash them in a separate bowl or with the sardines.
3. **Mix Ingredients:** In a large bowl, mix the mashed sardines, sweet peas, and chopped rosemary. Drizzle with olive oil.
4. **Blend for Consistency:** Use a hand blender or food processor to smooth the mixture to your preferred consistency.
5. **Serve or Store:** Serve the mash fresh, or store in airtight containers. Refrigerate for up to 3 days or freeze for up to a month.

BEEF AND BLUEBERRY BLEND

Ground beef mixed with antioxidant-rich blueberries

Protein: 65% | Fats: 25% | Carbohydrates: 8% | Minerals and vitamins: 2%

 10 min   32 oz   800 (25 per oz) kcal

INGREDIENTS

- 24 oz raw ground beef (preferably lean)
- 8 oz fresh blueberries

DIRECTIONS

1. **Prep Beef:** Purchase high-quality, lean ground beef. Ensure it's fresh and serve it raw safely.
2. **Prep Blueberries:** Wash the blueberries thoroughly under cold water. Pat them dry with a clean towel.
3. **Mix Ingredients:** Combine the ground beef and blueberries in a large mixing bowl. Use your hands or a spoon to gently mix the ingredients until the blueberries are evenly distributed throughout the beef.
4. **Serve or Store:** Serve this blend immediately or divide it into meal-sized portions. Store the portions in airtight containers. Refrigerate for up to 2 days or freeze for up to a month.

SALMON AND SWEET POTATO

Chopped salmon with nutrient-dense sweet potato

Protein: 60% | Fats: 30% | Carbohydrates: 8% | Minerals and vitamins: 2%

15 min	32 oz	640 (20 per oz) kcal

INGREDIENTS

- 16 oz raw salmon, deboned and finely chopped
- 16 oz sweet potatoes, peeled and grated

DIRECTIONS

1. **Pree Salmon:** Please make sure the salmon is fresh and sourced responsibly. Carefully debone and finely chop the salmon into small, manageable pieces for your dog.
2. **Prep Sweet Potatoes:** Peel the sweet potatoes and grate them using a medium-sized grater. Grating them helps ensure they are more digestible for your dog.
3. **Mix Ingredients:** Combine the finely chopped salmon with the grated sweet potatoes in a large mixing bowl. Mix thoroughly to ensure an even distribution of salmon and sweet potatoes.
4. **Serve or Store:** This meal can be served fresh or divided into meal-sized portions and stored in airtight containers. Refrigerate for up to 3 days or freeze for up to a month.

PORK AND PARSLEY PATTY

Minced pork formed into patties with fresh parsley

Protein: 55% | Fats: 40% | Carbohydrates: 2% | Minerals and vitamins: 3%

15 min	30 oz	750 (25 per oz) kcal

INGREDIENTS

- 24 oz raw pork, minced
- 6 oz fresh parsley, finely chopped
- Optional for binding (if cooking): 1 egg, beaten

DIRECTIONS

1. **Minced Pork:** Use lean pork cuts for lower fat. If the pork is not pre-minced, grind it yourself or have your butcher do it.
2. **Prep Parsley:** Wash and finely chop it for flavor and its breath-freshening properties.
3. **Mix Ingredients:** Combine minced pork and parsley in a bowl. If cooking, add a beaten egg to bind the patties.
4. **Form Patties:** Shape the mixture into even patties, about 1/2 inch thick.
5. **Serve Raw or Cooked:**
6. **Raw:** Serve raw for dogs on a raw diet, ensuring freshness and proper handling.
7. **Cooked:** Cook in a medium skillet for 4 minutes per side until done.
8. **Cool and Serve:** Allow patties to cool to room temperature before serving.
9. **Storage:** Refrigerate in an airtight container for up to 3 days or freeze for longer storage

MACKEREL AND SWEET PEA MASH

Mackerel and sweet peas mashed together for a hearty meal

Protein: 55% | Fats: 35% | Carbohydrates: 8% | Minerals and vitamins: 2%

15 min	32 oz	640 (20 per oz) kcal

INGREDIENTS

- 20 oz raw mackerel, deboned and finely chopped
- 12 oz sweet peas, cooked and cooled (if using frozen, thaw first)

DIRECTIONS

1. **Prep Mackerel:** Ensure the mackerel is fresh. Carefully debone and chop the fish into small, manageable pieces for your dog.
2. **Prep Sweet Peas:** If using frozen sweet peas, ensure they are completely thawed. Mash the peas lightly with a fork or potato masher until they reach a coarse consistency.
3. **Mix Ingredients:** Combine the finely chopped mackerel with the mashed sweet peas in a large bowl. Mix thoroughly to integrate the peas with the mackerel.
4. **Serve or Store:** Serve this mash fresh or divide it into meal-sized servings and store it in airtight containers. You can refrigerate the mash for up to 3 days or freeze it for up to a month.

SALMON AND CUCUMBER DICE

Diced salmon mixed with fresh cucumber

Protein: 60% | Fats: 30% | Carbohydrates: 8% | Minerals and vitamins: 2%

10 min	30 oz	450 (15 per oz) kcal

INGREDIENTS

- 20 oz raw salmon, deboned and finely diced
- 10 oz cucumber, peeled, deseeded, and diced

DIRECTIONS

1. **Prep Salmon:** Select fresh, high-quality salmon, remove all bones and skin, and dice into small, bite-sized pieces.
2. **Prep Cucumber:** Peel and halve the cucumber lengthwise, remove seeds, and dice into pieces like the salmon.
3. **Mix Ingredients:** In a bowl, mix the salmon and cucumber evenly.
4. **Serve Fresh:** Serve immediately to preserve the freshness and texture of the ingredients.
5. **Store:** If needed, refrigerate the mix in a sealed container for up to 24 hours; avoid freezing to maintain texture.

CHAPTER 5

HOW TO STRUCTURE YOUR FURRY FRIEND'S DIET

Dogs thrive on routine, so a consistent mealtime is key to keeping your furry friend healthy, happy, and well-behaved. In this chapter, we'll walk you through building a feeding schedule that fits your dog's unique needs. With a little planning, you'll help your pet avoid overeating, reduce tummy troubles, and stay on track with training.

5.1. WHY A FEEDING SCHEDULE MATTERS

- Dogs feel more secure and less anxious when meals are served regularly.
- Consistent meal times prevent overfeeding and help maintain a healthy weight.
- Regular meals promote better digestion and prevent upset stomachs.
- Scheduled feeding times are perfect for training and reinforcing good behavior.

5.2. STEPS TO CREATE A TAILORED FEEDING SCHEDULE

1. Figure Out Your Dog's Daily Calories:
- Calculate your dog's daily caloric needs based on weight, age, breed, and activity level.
- Adjust for special needs like pregnancy, lactation, or health conditions.

2. Pick the Number of Meals Per Day:
- Puppies: 3-4 meals a day to fuel their growth.
- Adults (1-7 years): 2 meals a day to keep them energized and healthy.
- Seniors (7+ years): 2-3 smaller meals daily to accommodate slower metabolisms.

3. Divide the Calories Between Meals:
- Spread your dog's daily calorie count across meals to give balanced nutrition throughout the day.

4. Set Consistent Mealtimes:
- Stick to the same daily meal times to create a predictable routine.
- Example: Breakfast at 7 AM and Dinner at 6 PM.

5. Include Treats and Snacks Wisely:
- Use treats for training and account for them in the daily calorie count.
- Healthy snacks like carrot sticks or apple slices can be offered between meals.

6. Monitor and Adjust:
- Keep an eye on your dog's weight and condition.
- Adjust portion sizes or meal frequency if needed.
- Consult your vet for advice on any special dietary needs.

5.3. SAMPLE FEEDING SCHEDULE

Puppy (8 weeks - 6 months):
- 7:00 AM: Breakfast (¼ of daily calories)
- 12:00 PM: Lunch (¼ of daily calories)
- 5:00 PM: Dinner (¼ of daily calories)
- 9:00 PM: Evening Meal (¼ of daily calories)

Adult Dog (1 - 7 years):
- 7:30 AM: Breakfast (50% of daily calories)
- 6:30 PM: Dinner (50% of daily calories)

Senior Dog (7+ years):
- 7:30 AM: Breakfast (40% of daily calories)
- 12:30 PM: Lunch (20% of daily calories)
- 6:30 PM: Dinner (40% of daily calories)

Special Considerations:
- Medical Conditions: Dogs with diabetes or tummy issues might need smaller, frequent meals.
- Active Dogs: Working or very active dogs may need extra snacks or an additional meal.
- Overweight Dogs: Trim portion sizes and avoid high-calorie treats.

5.4. TIPS FOR KEEPING YOUR SCHEDULE ON TRACK

- Meal Prep: Prepare meals ahead of time to make feeding easy.
- Automatic Feeders: Consider using automatic feeders for consistent meal times, especially if you're not home.
- Avoid Free-Feeding: Leaving food out all day can lead to overeating and weight gain.

A well-planned feeding schedule ensures your dog gets the right nutrition at the right times, helping it stay healthy and happy. With these tips, you can build a routine that works for both you and your pet.

CHAPTER 6

TIPS FOR PREPARATION AND STORAGE OF HOMEMADE DOG FOOD

Making your dog's meals from scratch is a wonderful way to ensure they get wholesome, nutritious ingredients. But to make the most of your efforts, it's essential to prepare and store the food properly. In this chapter, you'll find practical advice on how to prep efficiently, keep meals fresh, and make mealtime stress-free for you and your furry friend.

6.1. PREPARATION TIPS

1. Plan Your Menu:
- Create a weekly menu to stay organized and ensure balanced nutrition.
- Mix up different proteins, veggies, and grains to give your pup variety.

2. Batch Cooking is Your Friend:
- Cook large batches of food at once to save time.
- Portion out meals for the week ahead to streamline mealtimes.

3. Prep Ingredients in Advance:
- Wash, peel, and chop vegetables, then store them in airtight containers in the fridge.
- Measure out grains and keep them ready for quick cooking.

4. Use the Right Equipment:
- Food Processor/Blender: Quickly chop or puree ingredients.
- Slow Cooker/Instant Pot: Ideal for cooking large batches with minimal effort.
- Silicone Baking Mats: Make baking treats easy and mess-free.

5. Follow Safe Cooking Practices:
- Cook proteins thoroughly to avoid harmful bacteria.
- Avoid using ingredients that are toxic to dogs (like onions, garlic, and chocolate).
- Don't add salt, spices, or other seasonings.

6.2. STORAGE TIPS

1. Cool Food Quickly:
- After cooking, let the food cool to room temperature before storing.
- Divide into small portions to speed up the cooling process.

2. Refrigerate Correctly:
- Store in airtight containers or resealable bags.
- Label containers with the date to keep track of freshness.
- Refrigerated food should be used within 3-4 days.

3. Freeze for Longer Storage:
- Freeze batches in portion-sized containers or freezer bags.
- Label with the type of food and the date it was made.
- Use frozen meals within 2-3 months for optimal freshness.
- Thaw overnight in the fridge or use a microwave if you're in a hurry.

4. Store Treats Properly:
- Refrigerate fresh-baked treats in airtight containers for up to 2 weeks.
- Freeze extras to keep them fresh for up to 6 months.
- Consider using vacuum-sealed bags for longer shelf life.

5. Use Safe Containers:
- Glass, BPA-free plastic, or silicone containers are best.
- Avoid storing food in thin plastic bags, which can leak and allow odors to escape.

6.3. MEALTIME TIPS

1. Portion Control:
- Measure out the right amount for each meal based on your dog's size, age, and activity level.
- Use a kitchen scale or measuring cup to ensure consistent portions.

2. Warm It Up:
- Serve refrigerated or frozen food at room temperature.
- Warm up meals in the microwave for a few seconds or mix in a bit of hot water.

3. Add Supplements as Needed:
- Some vitamins and supplements are best added fresh before serving.
- Consult your vet for the right supplements for your pup's diet.

4. Rotate Recipes:
- Rotate different proteins, grains, and veggies for a balanced diet.
- Experiment with new ingredients to keep your dog's meals interesting.

Making homemade dog food is a labor of love and an art that requires more than just good ingredients. It also demands good preparation and storage practices to ensure your dog's safety. By following these tips, you'll keep your dog's meals fresh, nutritious, and delicious.

CHAPTER 7

SAMPLE 28-DAY NUTRITIONAL PLAN

7.1. HOW TO USE THIS PLAN

• **Customization:** Every dog is unique, so feel free to adjust portion sizes and ingredients according to your dog's size, age, activity level, and dietary preferences.

• **Consult Your Vet:** Before starting any new diet, consult with your veterinarian to ensure it meets your dog's specific needs.

• **Meal Rotation:** To avoid monotony, rotate proteins and vegetables. This will also provide a broader range of nutrients.

• **Supplements:** Consider adding supplements like omega-3s, probiotics, or glucosamine to meet additional nutritional needs

Tips for Success:

- • **Batch Cooking:** Prepare large batches and store individual portions in the freezer.
- • **Hydration:** Ensure your dog can always access fresh water.
- • **Treats and Snacks:** Integrate healthy treats like carrot sticks, apple slices (without seeds), or pumpkin bites.

Customizing the Plan

Every dog is different, so use the recipes and guidelines provided to mix and match according to your pet's preferences and dietary needs. Feel free to swap proteins (chicken for turkey, lamb for beef, etc.) and adjust portions for larger or smaller breeds.

So, you have a wide range of tools that you can use when creating dishes. By replacing food items in a meal (for example, replacing meat with fish or poultry or some vegetables with others, etc.), you can significantly increase the number of recipes and diversify your pet's diet.

Day	Breakfast	Dinner
1	Chicken and Rice Simmer	Simple Beef Stew
2	Turkey and Spinach Quick Fry	Tuna and Rice Fluff
3	Chicken Breast Strips	Pork and Spinach Mini Rolls
4	Salmon and Sweet Potato Mash	Chicken and Zucchini Sauté
5	Quail and Apple Mix	Liver and Apple Bites
6	Lamb and Cucumber Mix	Snapper and Spinach
7	Chicken and Cucumber Salad	Beef Patty Bake
8	Turkey Veggie Mash	Haddock and Carrot Bake

9	Bison Bites	Liver Vegetable Medley
10	Duck and Sweet Potato Bake	Turkey and Carrot Balls
11	Pollock and Parsley Pot	Ground Beef and Squash Casserole
12	Ground Lamb and Rice	Duck and Pumpkin Puree
13	Turkey and Pumpkin Cubes	Trout and Apple Mix
14	Beef and Egg Scramble	Chicken Heart Stew
15	Sardine and Pea Salad	Turkey and Rice Soup
16	Halibut and Rice Pilaf	Ground Beef and Carrot Soup
17	Chicken Liver and Zucchini Plate -	Simple Ground Venison
18	Turkey and Beet Blend	Catfish and Cucumber Cool Down
19	Meatloaf Minis	Chicken Gizzard Goulash
20	Bison and Beet Cubes	Duck and Carrot Sticks
21	Cod and Broccoli Bowl	Pumpkin Rice Delight
22	Liver and Pea Pilaf	Simple Venison Strips
23	Turkey Giblet Mix	Tilapia and Broccoli Mousse
24	Chicken and Apple Quick Cook	Beef and Carrot Tartare -
25	Lamb Broth Bowl	Duck and Pea Patties
26	Mackerel Patties	Chicken and Apple Raw Mix -
27	Pork and Kale Sauté	Salmon and Parsnip Patties
28	Sweet Potato and Lentil Loaf	Simple Chicken Liver Fry

A well-planned, homemade diet can remarkably impact your pet's health and happiness. With this 28-day plan, you're on your way to providing your furry friend with delicious, nutritious, balanced meals made with love. Your dog will thank you with wagging tails and wet-nosed gratitude!

CONCLUSION

The Joy and Benefits of Homemade Feeding

Thank you so much for embarking on this enriching journey with us through the delightful world of homemade dog food. As we close this cookbook, we wish you to feel not only inspired but also well-prepared to introduce the same level of care and love into your dog's meals as you would for any cherished member of your family.

The Case for Homemade: The advantages of homemade dog food are numerous and significant. The most important one is the complete control you have over the ingredients in your dog's diet. This means you can avoid unwanted preservatives, questionable meat sources, and potential allergens often found in commercial dog foods. By opting for fresh, wholesome ingredients, you can ensure your dog is thriving on nutritionally balanced meals.

Customized Nutrition: Another significant advantage is the ability to tailor your dog's diet to their unique nutritional requirements. Every recipe presented in this cookbook can be modified to cater to your dog's specific needs. Whether your pet requires a diet high in protein, low in carbohydrates, or perhaps needs a boost in certain vitamins, homemade meals make it easy to adjust their diet accordingly.

Strengthening Bonds Through Cooking: Preparing meals for your dog does more than feed them; it strengthens the emotional bond between you and your pet. The act of cooking for your dog is a demonstration of love and care, which enhances the connection you share. This experience is something that cannot be replicated with store-bought kibble.

Visible Health Benefits: Switching to homemade meals often leads to a noticeable improvement in your pet's overall health and vitality. Owners frequently report brighter eyes, a glossier coat, and a more consistent level of energy throughout the day. These changes are clear signs that your dog is thriving on its new diet, and they're a compelling reason to consider homemade dog food.

As you continue your homemade dog food journey, remember that patience and consistency are your best tools. It may take some time to discover the ideal recipes and portion sizes that best suit your dog's tastes and nutritional needs. Maintain regular consultations with your veterinarian, keep an eye on your dog's health, and adjust their diet as necessary. Your dedication to their health is a wonderful reflection of the special place they hold in your life.

We hope this cookbook becomes a valuable resource for crafting many nutritious and enjoyable meals for your treasured pet. Here's to a future filled with health, happiness, and countless joyful tail wags at mealtime!

Happy cooking, and even more joyful wagging!